16 Strategies for Sales
By Sean Moudry

Copyright ©2019
All Rights Reserved

Acknowledgements

I wish to first give recognition to my beautiful wife and children who have been so patient and supportive while I took family time to get these thoughts into words. Thank you is not enough to express my appreciation.

To my collaborator Kate Fey who, over the past five years, helped me develop each of the strategies through application and observation. This book would not have been possible without your passion for helping others. To Katie Cleveland, thank you for your commitment to the vision and the development of the website, book cover and graphic design. Thank you to my editor, Christina Tillitz, for taking countless hours to edit, rewrite and add additional content. And to Nicole Egtvedt for her entertaining drawings, thank you, they perfectly reflect my personality.

Thank you, Christine Beckwith, Jeff Zinsmeister and my friends at Annie-Mac Home Mortgage for giving me the encouragement to continue. Lastly, to my fearless coaching clients for being real and transparent. My hope is your honesty will help others find the best solutions for their success.

Thank you all,
          Sean

CONTENTS

Preface

Introduction 1

Section One: 16 Strategies for Sales

Chapter 1: One Size Doesn't fit All 6

Chapter 2: Finding Happiness and Success 11

Chapter 3: Forceful to Influential 15

Chapter 4: Habits, Beliefs, and Success 23

Chapter 5: Nature vs Nurture 37

Chapter 6: The Solution 44

Chapter 7: The Assessment 54

Chapter 8: Reviewing the Results and Strategy 56

Chapter 9: Awareness, Feedback and Accountability 66

Chapter 10: Working with Other Types 70

Chapter 11: Interactions Between Types 77

Chapter 12: 16 Strategies for Teams and Business 89

Chapter 13: Increasing Productivity 97

Chapter 14: Closing Thoughts 103

Section Two: 16 Strategies
Personality Types and Sales Strategies

Diplomat	107
Visionary	112
Advisor	117
Guide	124
Strategist	129
Debater	135
General	140
Entrepreneur	146
Authority	153
Contributor	159
Analyst	164
Operative	169
Advocate	175
Influencer	182
Guardian	186
Designer	192
About the Author	198

Preface

A note from the editor

Welcome to the next step toward achieving your desired success. This quick-read is packed with information on assessing personality types and how individual preferences can help, or impede, the journey toward reaching your full potential. Many of us struggle to find satisfaction in our careers, lives and relationships. We make progress, only to find ourselves back behind the starting line. We encounter people who frustrate and stifle us, who create stress and unhappiness. Why is there always that one coworker who makes us dread going to the office? The answer to enjoying success in your work, life and love — and appreciating grumpy coworkers — is not easy, but Sean has spent years making it simple enough to begin implementing right away. He has coached people across the United States and helped many of them realize the success of their dreams, often beyond any level of success he has personally achieved. But he is okay with this. Sean's drive comes from helping others reach their full potential. This book is for you.

Sean's 16 Strategies for Salespeople *identifies sixteen unique personality types and offers proven strategies to increase productivity for yourself, and your business. With multiple years of experience, and many bumps and bruises along the way, Sean shares what he has learned with honesty and humor. And just about the time you start to think he is the biggest jerk on the planet, keep reading. We can all identify with something in Sean's journey. He offers insight and quick maneuvers to avoid the many pitfalls encountered along the path toward success. Whether to just get us out the gate or down the whole road, Sean is here to help us reach our full potential and the level of success we desire.*

Enjoy!

INTRODUCTION

We all desire success, happiness and fulfillment. Isn't that what life is about? Pushing our limits, finding what we love and enjoying the experience along the way? When we start out, we sometimes struggle to find that sweet spot of a career we enjoy that also affords us a life we love. Oftentimes, we fall into an opportunity and start down a path toward our full potential. We push forward into what, at that time, feels like a version of our best life. We know life is never perfect, but at that given moment, we are satisfied. Yet, at some point, we begin to wonder if we might be happier doing other things. This feeling becomes more pronounced as we get older. Why is this? One reason is, as we make our journey through life, we are exposed to more options, and with experience and money more possibilities become available.

I began my real estate sales career in my early twenties. Looking back, I can say I was as happy as I could be. As my business grew, I began earning more money and meeting new people, which led to more experiences and opened up new opportunities. My new awareness of the great, big world around me quickly turned into "window shopping" different career paths and other possible avenues for success. I began to question myself: *Maybe I would be happier in a different field? Could I surpass my goals by going to the next level? How much more could I achieve by trying something new?*

I don't believe there is anything inherently wrong with exploring opportunities. We all desire to try new things and seek out new experiences. The trouble begins when we try new things and are not immediately successful, or maybe not successful at all. This was my experience. As new opportunities came my way and I took the leap of faith, I found myself in the completely new experiences of struggle, frustration and defeat. Today, I can sit here and tell you these aren't failures, they are lessons, but we humans get several failures under our belts and self-doubt has a sneaky way of getting in there as well. We begin to think there might be something wrong with us, that we might be— flawed.

This is a path I have traveled many times in my life. I have experienced massive success and I have experienced downright failure. I found myself wondering what was wrong with me. How could I be so naturally gifted at some things and so utterly incompetent at others?

This question led me on a journey to better understand human behavior. I began searching for a better understanding of myself. I have spent thousands of hours researching, reading and learning from some of the best performance experts in the world. I learned that I was not "fundamentally flawed," rather, it was the way I approached problems, and, the way I handled making decisions wasn't always right for the situation. I also learned I needed to work within my strengths and utilize my innate preferences, which, as you will learn, align with my natural abilities.

"How could I be so naturally gifted at some things and so utterly incompetent at others?"

I applied this new knowledge to the hundreds of real estate salespeople in my companies, as well as the national top producers I have personally coached. We customized sales strategies to the specific personality of each individual salesperson. No two people had the same plan. They were held accountable for their goals, but they had the freedom and flexibility to do it their own way. The results were outstanding! Sales increased, they experienced less stress, and best of all, they were happier.

The challenge with this approach is obvious. Who has the time and energy to customize a plan for each individual? We wanted an assessment that was accurate, yet easy to understand. We needed something that would help salespeople, leaders and teams implement individual strategies so they would start seeing results right away. While there are countless personality assessments available, none of them are uniquely geared toward sales.

Our solution was to create our own assessment based on the Myers-Briggs Type Indicator and to develop simple descriptions of each personality type to help you decide what sales strategy might be the most natural for your own innate preferences. The Myers-Briggs Type Indicator has sixteen psychological types, therefore, we developed our own "16 Strategies for Salespeople," offering sales strategies for each personality type.

To be effective in implementing the strategies presented in this book, you must first become self-aware and keep the new information top-of-mind. This requires keeping the lessons you have learned in front of you and implementing them often. Self-awareness is the key to change. Success and happiness come from awareness of our innate preferences and how they affect each aspect of our lives. This book is a tool to help you understand not only your own preferences, but also the preferences of others. It will allow you to become a better employee, coach, mentor or teacher. This is not a "read it once and put it on the shelf" book.

This book is intended to be a reference you can refer to often when dealing with customers, staff, colleagues, friends— and maybe even your spouse.

I found that a better understanding of myself, and of others, is the best path toward success, happiness and fulfillment. My goal throughout this book is for you to understand how to reach your full potential by learning your own innate preferences and embracing your natural gifts.

-Sean

CHAPTER 1
One Size Doesn't Fit All

Many self-help gurus suggest modeling others who have achieved what we wish to achieve. The definition of modeling in this case is acting like others through emulation or instruction. Typically, we find a mentor, a coach, or somebody who's influential in our life and we mimic what we see them do— emulation, or we do what they tell us to do— instruction.

However, we find that we might do the same activities they do, we may say the exact same things they say and act the same way they act, yet we do not achieve the success that they achieve. This is because we cannot duplicate the internal preferences and natural gifts our role models hold within themselves. Each person has their own set of guiding rules, their own way of collecting and prioritizing information and their own way of making decisions. When we model others, we have to understand how our own guidelines and preferences may differ from the person we are modeling.

Teachers, authors and coaches can only share from their own experiences and their unique perspective, they can't speak to yours. They show you the way they would do something or the way they would solve a problem from their individual point-of-view. Yet, we know through personal experience that don't all hold the same views, we don't all solve problems the same way or share the same motivations and we certainly don't make the same decisions or execute actions in the same way. We may find similarities, but we are all irrefutably different.

Consider public speaking, for example. It is a fairly universal perception that public speaking is either something you excel at or it makes you so uncomfortable you feel physically ill. Comedian Jerry Seinfeld famously said,

> *"According to most studies, people's number one fear is public speaking. Number two is death. Death is number two [...] This means, to the average person, if you go to a funeral, you're better off in the casket than delivering the eulogy."*

Why do some people have no problem with public speaking while others would rather die than open their mouths in front of a group of people?

In sales, there is a similar task that can cause many people to immediately start shopping for their headstones— "cold calls," or calls to people who are not expecting or did not request your call. Think back to the first time you had to make a cold call. What emotions did you experience? Did you think of the call as an outstanding opportunity or a violation of people's rights? Working with thousands of salespeople over twenty years has taught me that even if I convince people it is in their best interest to make cold calls, once left to work under their own supervision, most will not continue to make these calls. Why?

Many people choose sales as a career because they like being around people. It is a common feeling that soliciting by phone is an intrusion, one that violates values or other people's trust, which causes internal conflict. This conflict presents itself as fear, anxiety and stress. Your investment in training someone whose natural abilities are not going to motivate them to make cold calls is a waste of time and energy for both of you. If what your business needs is someone who will consistently make cold calls, a better understanding of human behavior will help you attract people with the internal preferences that will be most effective for your expectations, and it will help you place the person who is not comfortable making cold calls into a strategy that is a better fit for their personality. It is my belief that anyone can be successful at sales if they follow a strategy that aligns with their innate preferences.

Many companies spend hundreds of thousands of dollars on assessments to find the magic personality combination for building a successful sales team. In my experience, there are hundreds, if not thousands, of ways to achieve this goal. Most companies focus on a narrow personality type that has been blessed with a natural gift for sales. But, we can all agree that some personalities are more likely to be successful at typical sales strategies. You will see throughout this book how personalities that are not naturally sales-oriented can also achieve success in sales. The key is not to find the rare diamond in the coal, but to find the best way to turn the coal into diamonds.

If you are unhappy with what you are doing, or even the business you've created, consider the possibility that you are simply operating outside of your innate preferences. Imagine if there was a strategy you could apply, one in which you worked in alignment with your natural abilities, to achieve your desired success. This book is a guide for you to learn about other perspectives and preferences, and to help you, and your team, find success, happiness and fulfillment.

Reflection

What behaviors have you adopted through modeling others?

Have you been able to successfully replicate them?

Is there a task required in your job that you would rather not do?

To what degree of panic does it cause you?

CHAPTER 2
Finding Happiness and Success

There is no one-size-fits-all master plan for success. It is up to each of us to define our own happiness. I believe a universal key to happiness is to feel progress toward the objectives we desire. If we move closer each day to what we have individually defined as success, we feel happy. When we get stuck or feel we are moving farther away from our goals, we are less energized, less focused and less motivated.

When we feel this lack of progress we often ask ourselves, "What's wrong with me?" We begin to think there is an internal flaw that only exists within us, like a computer with bad wiring. This thinking can lead us to believe we need to change our own wiring. Learned and experiential behaviors can be modified and reprogrammed over time, but our innate preferences, our internal wiring, does not change. We can act outside of our innate preferences for a period of time but, eventually, we fall back. When this happens, we ask ourselves once again, "What's wrong with me?" We might also ask, "How do I fix it?" These are not valuable questions. To avoid this question trap, you need to insert new programming that works in concert with your internal wiring. Stop asking yourselves why you are wired the way you are and, instead, ask yourself "How can I be successful, happy and less stressed with the wiring I have

Merriam-Webster says happiness is a state of well-being and contentment, or joy. Think about it, what makes you happy? We often look to see what other people have and compare it against ourselves to determine our self-worth and happiness. I often have to remind top producers that there is no scoreboard in the sky. Nobody, outside of their company, is keeping track of their wins and losses, it is only in their minds. If they focus more on the goal, desire and challenge that truly matters to them, they will receive satisfaction greater than possessions or money. They will receive fulfillment.

If you are not currently getting the results you desire, take a moment to consider that you may not have tried the right approach to become successful in your current career. You may be working, at least in part, outside of your preference.

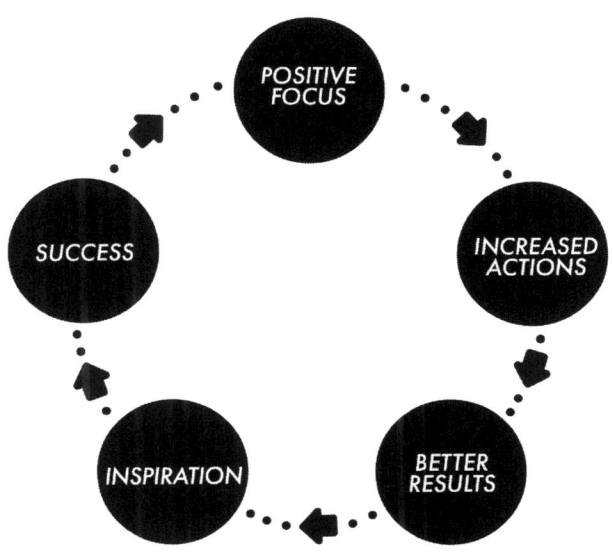

The Success Cycle

    When we focus on areas where we are naturally gifted, we find tasks easier. We may even find enjoyment in our work again. When we enjoy what we do, we naturally want to do more. When we are proactive and take more action, we see more results. And when we achieve the results we desire, we are inspired. This inspiration makes us want to repeat these same actions and, over time, we find success.

Reflection

What is your personal definition of success?

Do you feel you are moving toward it, away from it, or are your stuck?

In what areas of your work do you feel most satisfied?

What areas are most frustrating?

CHAPTER 3
Forceful to Influential

Early in my career, I only had to focus on my own wants, needs and desires. My goals were also focused on my own wants, needs and desires. All I had to do was wake up, get myself to work and continue to focus on my own success. I was not concerned with the ideas, desires or needs of the people around me, I was not responsible for them. If they were not satisfied with my perspective, I simply shrugged them off as misinformed.

As I became more successful, I wanted to be more influential. I wanted people to not only listen to me, but wholeheartedly agree with what I had to say. Someone who had achieved as high a level of success as I had would have influence over other people simply because of their status, right?

Boy, was I was wrong. Here is where that feeling flawed thinking came in. If other people didn't agree with me, I felt it was because I wasn't smart or good enough. If I couldn't convince them to see things from my perspective, then something must be wrong with me. I found myself at odds with friends, arguing about how they chose to spend their money or how I spent my free time. My wife and I disagreed on the simplest things, like what time was the right time to arrive at the airport. When I was confronted by others, I locked horns and pushed back like an elk in a clash over territory. I felt that if they would just see it my way, life would be easier. I would have less distractions and chaos. Needless to say, I was not always Mr. Congeniality.

Have you ever experienced ongoing conflict with another person that led you to think your life would be easier without them? Then, when they were not around, you longed for their company? Maybe you even missed the little things about them that used to drive you crazy. Think of relationships you may have lost over the years. Is there an exceptional employee that refuses to work with you, or family members that dread the controversy that often shows up with you? How about a long-time friend that just doesn't call anymore?

What would life look like if we had the ability to choose to shrug it all off and shut out the naysayers. If we just stood there, like Neo in *The Matrix*, watching offending comments and judgements fly past us like bullets as we calmly twist out of the way with a smile on our face. We would be unstoppable. Instead we are busy defending our own position. We don't listen to our inner truth telling us to back up and get out of our own way.

Fast forward to my early thirties. I'm married, with toddlers, and running a highly successful real estate business. I was in constant interaction with demanding customers, employees and a strong-minded business partner. Each day felt more difficult than the day before. Why wouldn't customers just listen to my advice without judgement or pushback. I had been selling real estate for nearly ten years and had sold hundreds of homes. *I had arrived!* However, despite this success I was not happy. My employees needed constant direction and emotional support and my business partner only chose to be involved when he could point out what he would have done differently.

I would come home exhausted to my kids playing quietly and a wife who understood all my troubles and helped me feel all my efforts were worth it (you're not buying that are you?). I came home to a wife and kids that longed for my attention. My wife's day was also hectic. She needed me to take the restless kids off her hands for a moment because moms don't get breaks when dads are at work. To my toddlers I had been gone, like forever. They were thrilled I was home and just wanted my undivided attention. These were not unreasonable requests, but I was so spent from work I had nothing left. I was stressed out and frustrated and my wife and I were angry and arguing.

There came a point when I could no longer bear the pressure. I literally walked away from the real estate business I had spent over a decade building. I wanted no more demanding customers, no big-headed business partner, no needy employees. I was annoyed that others still wouldn't respect me and just listen to my direction. It took this complete loss of everything I had worked so hard to build to realize my frustration was not coming from others, it was coming from within myself. It was coming from my judgement of just about everybody in my life. The more I wanted them to see the world through my eyes, the more aggravated I got when they didn't.

It took some genuine soul-searching for me to understand that in order to experience true happiness and fulfillment, I had to stop judging others for not seeing things from my point-of-view. I had to stop insisting they operate from my world. I had to learn to appreciate individual differences and to accept that good could come from other people's points-of-view.

After some serious sulking, I embarked on a new career that led me to a position as a Team Leader at one of the largest real estate brokerages in Denver, Colorado. This job required me to work directly with many different personalities. My main focus was to build relationships with real estate agents outside the company in order to gain influence and recruit them into my brokerage. Once they joined, my job was to train them to be top producers like I once was. I was certain I could perform this task, I had been one of the highest producing agents in the nation for over ten consecutive years.

Nine months into my new career and, guess what? I was failing miserably. I had already quit once because one of the owners told me I wasn't doing it the way she would (the nerve!). It took a lot of convincing, but I was rehired. Six months later I had recruited a total of zero, yes zero, producing real estate agents. It wasn't for a lack of trying. I had a simple, infallible plan:

Step 1: Set up an appointment.
Step 2: Tell them all about me.
Step 3: They sign up!

It was a great plan!

I mean, who wouldn't sign up to get the chance to work with me, one of the top producing agents in the nation. I lived the success they so much desired. All they needed to do was exactly what I told them, exactly the way I would do it and say exactly what I had been saying for ten straight years and they would, no doubt, be as successful as I was.

I can see you cringing. It became clear to me that my resume may have gotten their attention, but it didn't give me permission to tell them what to do. Even worse was the resentment I felt for the agents I was training. I was pouring all my energy into them, handing them every solution, every strategy. I removed every roadblock like a controlling helicopter parent at a parent-teacher conference, the one who knows more than all the teachers combined. And yet, no one, not one single agent, achieved the success I had achieved. Or at least, they didn't in the way I wanted them to. I had fallen back into the same trap of expecting others to duplicate my behaviors, my beliefs and my experiences.

To achieve my goals for my company, for my finances and for my own confidence, I had to find a solution that worked. I needed to learn to attract others without expecting them to follow me simply because I had an impressive resume. I wanted people to come to me because they believed I could help them, that I cared enough to understand what they were going through and that I could listen, without contempt. They needed to believe they could say anything, even if it didn't align with my beliefs or personal preferences, without my judgment.

I took a high-dive leap into every book, podcast and video I could find on human behavior, habits and psychology. The journey taught me that our innate preferences control our thoughts, and that our thoughts ultimately control our behaviors. When we understand our innate preferences, we are freed from trying to follow the one-size-fits-all influence style. If we want to be influential, we need to flex to understand other perspectives without shame, and without judgement.

This perspective has awarded me the opportunity to meet with, and influence, some of the most talented sales people across the country, as well as develop talented sales people within my own organization. It has helped me to better understand my own behaviors, beliefs and innate preferences, which has made me a better leader, a better husband and a better father. More than anything else, I have learned to stop judging and shaming myself when things don't go as planned. I can honestly say I am happier, more influential and more successful. I am an all-around better version of myself— and you can be, too.

Reflection

In what ways have you been judging others for not being like you?

Have you found yourself wanting to be more influential?

Have you seen yourself repeating ineffective, or unhealthy, patterns in your life?

CHAPTER 4
Habits, Beliefs and Success

There are a thousand-and-one books on how to achieve success, so I won't bore you with rehashed versions of the same old sales philosophies. But, to not acknowledge the following influences on success would be irresponsible. To reach your full potential you must become aware of the three areas that control your thoughts, feelings, behaviors and ultimately, your results. These are your habits, your beliefs and your innate preferences.

Habits

In the book, *The Power of Habit* (yes, you should read this book), author Charles Duhigg demonstrates that our habitual behaviors not only operate outside of our awareness but also control ninety-nine percent of the decisions we make on a daily basis. If we believe this is true (and I do) then we must become aware of our habitual behaviors. To do this, we must desire, request and enjoy feedback. Sounds easy, right? Wrong. Honestly, does anyone ever enjoy receiving feedback?

A few years ago, I was binge-watching a television series and one of the characters kept saying "At the end of the day" before every sentence. One afternoon, my wife said to me, "Why do you keep saying, "At the end of the day"? You are driving me crazy." I didn't even know I was saying it. Of course, after she brought it to my attention, I started to drive myself crazy. To change this behavior I had to re-train my speech. Each time I heard myself start the phrase I would pause and restart the sentence. Once this was brought into my awareness, I was able to correct the behavior and break the habit.

At the age of thirty-six, I was handed an "opportunity" that changed my life. Always tall and muscular, and a relatively healthy eater, health was the least of my concerns. Needless to say, I was blind-sided when I was diagnosed with a rare disease that caused my pancreas to stop producing insulin. This disease caused me to become Diabetic. When you are diagnosed with "the sugars," the doctor prescribes you the necessary medication and instructs you to meet with a nutritionist to help modify your diet. When meeting with a nutritionist, the first question they always ask is, "What is your diet?" I explained I had always been a relatively healthy eater. I failed to mention that I had just consumed three Krispy Kreme doughnuts right before my glucose test. I truly believed my diet was healthy because I didn't understand what a healthy diet actually was. My nutritionist didn't ask me to change my diet, she didn't even judge me for eating doughnuts when I finally confessed. She just told me to write down everything, and she meant everything, I put into my body. Every glass of water, every sandwich, every piece of cheesecake at dinner. She then scheduled for us to meet in a week to review my actual diet. By day three of tracking my food consumption, I could already see I was nowhere near the "relatively healthy eater" I thought myself to be. For one thing, I was eating five to ten times the amount of carbohydrates my body actually needed. Because of this new awareness of the types of food I was consuming, I began making adjustments to my diet even before my appointment. That is the power of feedback.

Tracking and measuring the actions we take toward our goals exposes the lies we tell ourselves about our progress. Our minds keep us happy by making us believe we are accomplishing more than we actually are, or could be. Keeping track of our efforts, and the results of those efforts, will allow us to improve.

Habits are not identified by any test or assessment. They can only be observed through our own awareness or from feedback through external observation. Feedback comes in many forms, such as customer reviews, employee reviews, comments and criticism, and, you guessed it, tracking. Feedback is often rejected because it forces us to look at our insecurities, behaviors and blind spots. But, learning to accept feedback allows us to adapt our behaviors and become aware and accepting of our imperfections. By opening ourselves up to feedback we make a conscious effort to improve and we become more willing to address our shortcomings.

Working with a coach is an effective way to conquer undesirable habits and identify tools you can employ to develop new, more beneficial habits. A coach also provides accountability by holding *attention to your intentions.* Without feedback we cannot grow, and without growth, we do not innovate.

Have you been made aware of a tic or habit you truly didn't know you had?

What ineffective habits are you aware of that you would like to change?

What types of feedback are you willing to accept?

What will you commit to today?

Beliefs

Beliefs are the rules that run our lives. Think of beliefs as programming on a computer. The computer will run any program you put into it and allows you to be productive. But, if a program turns out to be a virus, it will give you poor results and could permanently damage your computer and any other computer you have linked to your network. Beliefs are the programming that runs on the operating system of your unconscious mind.

Beliefs are formed in three ways: generational, experiential and unspoken. The most recognizable is generational. If we have been told our entire lives that something is true, we often assume it is true. We have all heard that ulcers are caused by stress, but did you know, in Australia in 1982, Dr. Robin Warren and Dr. Barry Marshall discovered that patients with ulcers also had a bacterium called *helicobacter pylori* present in their stomach that could be treated with antibiotics, and when treated the patient's ulcer would heal? One would think the medical field would be excited to hear these results. But, at that time, bacteria were not believed to live in the stomach. Dr. Warren said, "The wider medical community remained hard to convince" due to the generational belief that ulcers were caused by stress. It wasn't until 1997 that the Centers for Disease Control and Prevention developed a program to spread awareness that ulcers could be successfully treated with antibiotics. It took fifteen years for the generational beliefs about ulcers to change. In 2005, twenty-three years after their initial discovery, Robin Warren and Barry Marshall were awarded the Nobel Prize in Physiology or Medicine. Some generational beliefs can take decades, even generations, to overcome.

Can you identify generational beliefs that are preventing you from achieving your full potential?

Experiential beliefs, on the other hand, are formed from our own experiences. It is common knowledge that the stock market fluctuates up and down, and you may have heard someone say they won't invest in the stock market because they did one time and they lost money. However, if you look at the overall picture of the stock market, you will see that it consistently rises over time. Logic should then tell you that diversifying stocks (or, not putting all of your ducks in one row) and time can prevent you from losing money. Yet, if someone believes they will lose money investing in the stock market, that belief drives their decisions and becomes their reality. When the stock market drops, they may panic and decide to pull their money out thinking they will only lose more money as the market continues to fall. They don't take into consideration the fact that, historically, the stock market has proven to consistently rise over time. If they believed there was a way to always make money in the stock market, they would continue to look for, and respond to, different cues to make better decisions about how they invest.

Unfortunately, when an experience is so painful, we reject any other perspective. Prior to the recession in the late 2000s I had accumulated several rental properties. Like others, I was also speculating on luxury properties. When the recession hit, I not only lost value in my properties, my personal income dropped because home sales plummeted, as well. The experience of the recession and dealing with the pain of losing properties to foreclosure left me with such a bad taste in my mouth that I refused to invest again when the real estate market returned. It wasn't that I didn't see the opportunity, it was simply that the thought of investing again brought up all the emotions I associated with the prior experience. The result was, while my friends and colleges acquired millions, I missed out on possibly the best opportunity in my lifetime to invest in real estate.

Are you holding on to experiential beliefs that are no longer serving you?

Unspoken beliefs are the most difficult to uncover. These beliefs are like a wound that is wrapped in bandages, encased in a cast, then covered in armor. We often protect our unspoken beliefs out of the fear of being exposed or hurt by others. We may even keep them hidden so deep we forget they exist. However, they can still prevent us from achieving our full potential, from being our most authentic self and operating from where we are most productive. In his book, *The Big Leap* (yes, read this one, too), Gay Hendricks refers to unspoken beliefs as the four barriers of achievement.

The belief that you are inherently damaged. This **"fundamentally flawed"** belief prevents you from reaching your full potential and obtaining what you truly desire. Because you believe you are fundamentally flawed, you do not put in a full effort because if you do, you are destined to fail and everyone will see the truth— that you are not good enough, smart enough or talented enough. So instead of giving your full effort, you choose to play small so when you fail, you fail small and you can say you didn't really try. This way nobody knows your secret, that you are fundamentally flawed.

Carol Dweck discusses the difference between a fixed mindset and a growth mindset in her book, *Mindset* (read it!). The fear of failure is commonly caused by the belief that characteristics such as intelligence, skills, talent and beauty are the qualities we are born with and cannot be learned or improved. This is a **fixed mindset**. If we give maximum effort— on a test, a new venture or in our job— and we fail, it proves we were not made as intelligent, skilled or talented as those who succeed. A **growth mindset** is not so much that you are learning-based, but more so that you are willing to take chances and accept failure. The growth mindset believes that intelligence, skills and talent are all things that are developed through intentional practice and application. Failure is simply part of the process in developing characteristics you desire.

Will you accept failure as a stepping stone?

Will you allow failures to become your mile markers on the road to your success and happiness?

Will you choose to believe in yourself and give it your full effort?

    The belief of being disloyal. This belief is the mindset that you cannot stray from tradition or family expectations. You believe that if you choose a path outside your family's ideals, you will be a disappointment and alienate your loved ones.

    You might not know her name but you have heard of Stefani Joanne Angelina Germanotta. Her greatest desire was to be a classical musician. Her parents wanted her to become a doctor. She promised her parents that if she was not successful pursuing her musical career after one year, she would return to medical school. Today she has hundreds of music awards including 3 Academy Awards and was nominated for Best Actress for her role in A Star is Born. She is professionally known as Lady Gaga. What if Lady Gaga followed the belief that becoming a musician would be disloyal to her family, would she be happy today as a doctor? "Paging Dr. Gaga." Instead, she followed her heart, her innate preferences, and is touching lives through her music.

Who do you feel you are being disloyal to by following your dreams?

Will you let go of the belief you are being disloyal by achieving your dreams?

The belief that success brings a bigger burden. This belief comes in two parts. The first is the belief that chasing your dreams places a burden on those around you, and second, that as you expand to your full potential, your business will become a bigger burden on yourself or your loved ones.

In the film *Rudy*, Rudy Ruettiger's father pressures him to stop pursuing his dream, telling him, "Chasing a stupid dream causes you and everyone around you heartache." Rudy's father speaks from his past. As Rudy reaches closer to his dream, his father must deal with pain he experienced in his own childhood. Rudy feels the more he pursues his goal, the more pain he inflicts on his father. Rudy's father must come to terms with his pain in order to support Rudy in chasing his dream.

As your business grows and you achieve greater success, the demand on your time and money also increases. For most people, time and money are already scarce, so the fear of having even less is terrifying. Yet, we know that anything worth pursuing is going to take time, if not both time and money. It all comes down to the decision of priorities. I find it interesting that the same people who say they don't have the money to pay for a class or upgrade to more efficient software are often the same ones carrying the latest Apple products and a venti-sized Starbucks.

Before fulfilling his dream of selling the screenplay to the movie *Rocky*. Sylvester Stallone was so broke he sold his dog for $25. After Stallone sold the movie, he purchased his dog back for $15,000! I believe it was the great philosopher Friedrich Nietzsche who said "He who has a 'why' to live can bear almost any 'how.'" In other words, when you believe in your goal, you will make sacrifices and find the necessary resources.

We may also fear that reaching our full potential may require us to hire or manage people. This fear prevents us from growing. Fortunately, there are many options, such as technology or outsourcing, to help tackle the aspects of your business where you may not feel comfortable, such as accounting, graphic design or even lead generation. Many successful people have found that a partnership allows them to continue to focus on their strengths while their partner tackles other aspects, such as managing employees and the sales team.

Are you willing to sell your dog to reach your dreams?

Is your "why" big enough to overcome the "how?"

Are you going to continue to let excuses get in your way?

The belief of outshining others. This is the worry that if you reach your full potential, you may outshine others (siblings, family, partner, spouse) and this could make them feel that they are not good enough. They may feel abandoned, or flawed, and you don't anyone to feel bad about themselves.

I have unfortunately experienced this myself. I have a brother that is four years my senior and a sister that is fifteen years my junior. I identify with my sister more as a father figure than an older sibling. My brother, on the other hand, has experienced me as a rambunctious, ambitious and demanding little brother that always seemed to get his way. My brother and I have different fathers, but despite his father being taller than mine, I grew as tall as my brother by the time I was in fourth grade. People always thought we were twins. I have a preference toward extroversion to his introversion, so I found it easier to make friends. Parents believed in the 1980s that all children should be outside and social, so our mother often sent my brother outside the play with me and the neighborhood kids. This created a kind of social dependence on me. Since he didn't have many friends, he needed me to help him gain, and sometimes manage, his friendships. Fast forward twenty years and I was still the one coordinating and managing relationships for both of us. Over time, he began to resent my new friendships and felt they took priority over him and his family. Ultimately, our relationship grew apart and, despite my efforts, we have not spoken for several years.

It's not easy to admit, but I often worry about allowing myself to shine and how it might affect the people I love. It took time, but I have learned to recognize this belief, so when it raises its ugly head, I can affirm it away into oblivion.

> *"...we spend most of our time trying to win over the haters and the neutrals and as a result we become invisible to our tribe, and they*

can't find us, because we are not willing to shine our light. You can't control what others do but we can control shining our light so our tribe can find us. We must trust that there will be people there to receive us when we do shine our light."
-Amy Pearson, Blogger

Are you willing to stop worrying about others and choose to shine your light so your tribe can find you?

Do you believe it is not only our right, but our duty to expand to our full potential?

Do you agree to continue to expand to your full potential despite failure, money, time and the fear of outshining others?

CHAPTER 5
Nature vs Nurture

Innate preferences are more closely related to our unique personality. It is these preferences that may differ from our immediate family or people of influence. We often recognize our innate preferences through repetitive behaviors or from results we consistently receive in our life experiences.

If you're a parent of more than one child or have siblings, you have likely experienced the unique behaviors of humans. One child is born strong-willed and tenacious while the other is calm and patient. Both children have the same parents, both have similar, if not the same, experiences, they receive the same guidance and discipline, yet they act and react completely different. As they grow, these behavioral traits do not change.

The philosopher, Plato, believed we have impersonal and inherited traits that present and motivate human behavior before any consciousness develops. Simply put, Plato taught that we all have specific personality and behavior traits that are encoded at birth and do not change based on our experiences. We can move closer to and further from our innate preferences, but we cannot escape them.

When Helen always stands at the back of the room at conferences there isn't any prior experience that makes her stand behind the crowd, she just prefers it there. It stems from the part of her personality that is reserved. She was likely the child who was calm and patient. While her sister, who is at the front of the room with a captive audience, was the child who was strong-willed and tenacious.

Think of it like honey bees that are encoded with duties and responsibilities in order for the colony to survive. Humans also contain the encoding that allows the continued success of our species. What would happen if a colony of bees only collected pollen while none were left to build and guard the hive? The colony would be quickly overtaken by honey-craving bears.

Colonies and communities require different skills, interests and beliefs to function. It is nature's version of checks and balances.

Have you ever found yourself repeating the same story, such as a negative experience at a job, only to find ourselves right back in a similar scenario? Same experience, different job? Have you heard the quote from the film, *The Adventures of Buckaroo Banzai in the 8th Dimension*, "Wherever you go, there you are"? It's funny, but it is true. We bring our behaviors, our preferences and our decision-making processes with us wherever we go, which speaks to our tendency to repeat the same patterns. Repeating the same patterns will produce similar results, even if they are negative. By identifying these patterns, we can gain insight into the way we make decisions, where we are gifted or naturally skilled and where we are ineffective. In turn, this self-discovery helps us to better understand others and to accept their innate preferences, their behaviors and their strengths and weaknesses, without judgement or frustration.

Our personal experiences also play an important role in the way we behave. Therefore, it is important to separate innate preference from our learned or experiential behaviors. If Paul says he won't eat dinner at a specific restaurant because the last time he ate there, the food was awful, this does not come from an innate preference in which Paul believes all restaurant food is disgusting. It is an experiential behavior caused by a single incident at that particular restaurant.

Experiential behavior can also be handed down from family preferences or adopted beliefs based on a person of influence. Mary comes from a family of musicians. Her parents required their children to learn at least one musical instrument. Mary chose to play the piano because it was the one instrument she didn't have to haul to and from school every day. Mary is a gifted pianist, but while she enjoys the time spent with her parents on tours, she internally desires to be an architect and experiment with cutting edge design. Mary would prefer not to play the piano, but because music has always been at the center of her life, she continues to play more out of an ingrained family obligation rather than her own desire. This is an experiential behavior that has been handed down through tradition or unspoken family rules.

Modeling is another form of experiential behavior. We make choices based on what we have seen in the actions or belief system of someone we deem influential. Many experiential decisions are easy to spot, that is, we can trace a connection between the behavior and an outside source. A son dresses like his father, a new sales person who mimics speech patterns of her mentor and a daughter who studies music because she loves her parents are all examples of experiential behaviors.

Understand that we may have past experiences that have affected us in ways which are not easily identified. It may take some soul searching to dig deep enough to find what influences some of our behaviors. There is a saying that the reason Tiger Woods has a coach is because he cannot see himself swing a golf club. This is also true with behaviors. We are not always aware of our own behaviors because they are so natural to us. Sharing with a trusted friend, coach or therapist and jotting down our experiences, or journaling, can influence our ability to identify key behaviors or trigger points.

By reflecting on our experiences, we can gain an understanding of why we may act a certain way or make certain decisions in any given situation. These experiences can be positive or negative. This same type of reflection can be applied to a person who may be frustrating you. While I am not promoting digging into other people's past in order to figure out what is causing them to behave the way they do, you may know that Brent's wife was in a car accident or Julia is new to working in a big city and these external factors can influence their behavior.

Innate preferences may be more subtle. James can't understand why every company he has worked for has promoted him to management when he would rather not be in charge. It is likely that James is a competent decision maker and has a natural tendency to direct people. This is an innate internal preference because it shows up repeatedly in his career choices. James may not believe he would be a good leader, but something in his personality conveys the desire and proficiency to lead. Others immediately recognize this in James ability to quickly promote him to leadership positions.

The key takeaway here is, it is up to you to identify your own personal behaviors in order to achieve results. Your goal is to create an atmosphere of understanding and acceptance as if your success depends on it. Because it does. This unconscious behavior, our innate programming, is what drives us to do what we do and influences why and what we believe. It either aids us, or undermines our progress toward success, happiness and fulfillment.

Reflection

Have you noticed a trait or behavior in yourself that cannot be explained by an experience? What is it?

In what area of your life do you excel so far beyond others, that it is like having a superpower?

What areas in your life are you unskilled or feel completely incompetent?

CHAPTER 6
The Solution

Early in my leadership career we were taught to do a personality assessment on each person in my organization. I found the assessments to be a useful tool for developing relationships, but not quite as helpful for training and coaching. The sales organization I worked for utilized the DiSC profile. They were interested in hiring the personality type listed on this profile as "Dominant." The Dominant personality is described as "motivated by winning, competition and success." They are driven, self-confident, accept challenges and take action. This personality type would be a natural for sales, right? Not necessarily, although many companies still focus on hiring employees with these traits.

After doing countless DiSC validations and hundreds of hours training and coaching, I felt something was missing. If a Dominant personality is results oriented it would seem they should have no trouble making sales calls. Yet, I found that many were not willing to make even one sales call. My personal DiSC profile listed Dominant and Influence as my main types. Looking back at my own sales career I realized, even I had never made sales calls. Additionally, I have met Dominant personality types that were not successful at sales. So, if being Dominant does not guarantee top performance, why do so many sales organizations emphasize hiring this personality type? I had to find the answer.

A quick search online will give endless results for personality assessments. There are "14 Free Personality Tests You Can Take Today," and "The Best Personality Tests In Ranking Order (2019 Edition)," which lists twenty-two different tests. My expertise, and the basis of this book, draws from the three more prominent personality assessments— The DiSC profile, the Myers-Briggs Type Indicator and the Keirsey Temperament Sorter.

DiSC Profile

This profile was developed by physiological psychiatrist, William Moulton Marsten, PhD. The DiSC Model of Behavior was first introduced in Marsten's book, *Emotions of Normal People*, which was first published in 1928. Marsten studied, "the concepts of will and a person's sense of power and their effect on personality and human behavior." Marsten theorized that emotions contributed to behavioral differences and questioned how behavior might change over time. The four types on the DiSC profile are:

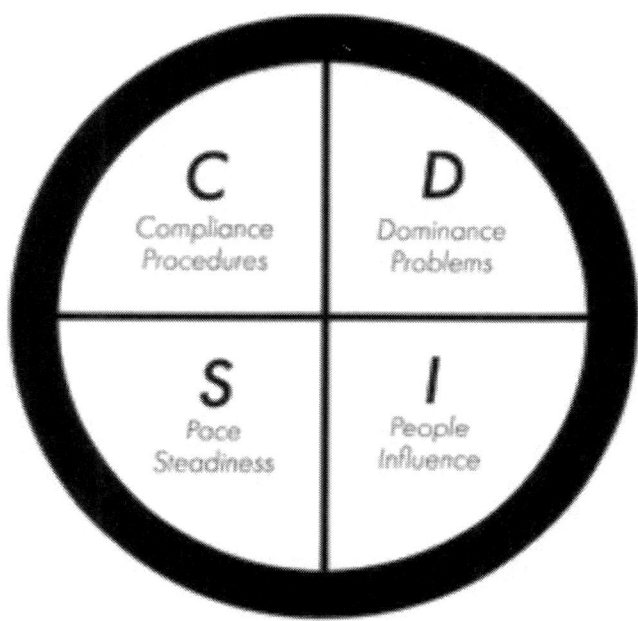

D- Dominant (Dominance)*
i- Inducement (Influence)*
S- Submissive (Steadiness)*
C- Compliance (Conscientiousness)*
  *parenthesis indicate 2007 updated terms.

The primary drawback to this profile is its focus on observable traits. Is the subject going to exhibit a dominant behavior? Are they going to prefer detailed analysis over simplification? Are they likely to fear rejection? This profile is used worldwide and by hundreds of companies. However, I wanted to dig deeper into the layers of human behavior and experience. This assessment gave me the *what*, I wanted to understand the *why*.

Myers-Briggs Type Indicator

The need to understand different behaviors led me to the Myers-Briggs personality research. Katharine Cook Briggs worked to create a formulation to understand the root of human behavior and the differences. In 1923, Katharine found Dr. Carl Jung's book, *Psychological Types* (1921), to be a comprehensive resource on psychological types and continued her own research based on Jung's findings. Dr. Jung based his research on the writings of Greek philosopher, Plato, taking these ideas farther to create sixteen personality profiles that categorized individual preferences. Plato observed that humans share unique qualities also found in other animal species, particularly species that live in colonies. Similar to bees and ants, humans tend to have preferences toward behaviors and decisions that are innate in nature. Jung suggested that when a person's environment is working against his nature he responds with disagreement, frustration and anger. Katharine Briggs wanted individuals to not only understand, but to also appreciate differences "to enhance harmony and productivity in diverse populations."

During World War II, Katharine's daughter, Isabel Briggs Myers, in doing her part to support the war effort, utilized her mother's research to analyze personality types and help women choose war-time jobs for which they were best suited and where they would be most effective. Prior to this, most women did not work outside the home. Isabel's work helped place many women in industrial jobs that kept the country running while most of America's workers fought the Axis powers overseas. After the war, this same process helped women find new work based on their innate preferences.

Isabel went on to create the questionnaire now known as the Myers-Briggs Type Indicator (MBTI). This assessment continues to be extensively researched to provide the clearest understanding of individual, innate preferences. The MBTI identifies four areas of preference:

The MBTI assessment allows for a quick analysis of a subject's innate preference. After a subject completes the assessment, it should be validated to ensure the subject had a clear understanding of description and vocabulary. After the validation, the subject will have a better understanding of their innate preferences, as well as insight into the innate preferences of others.

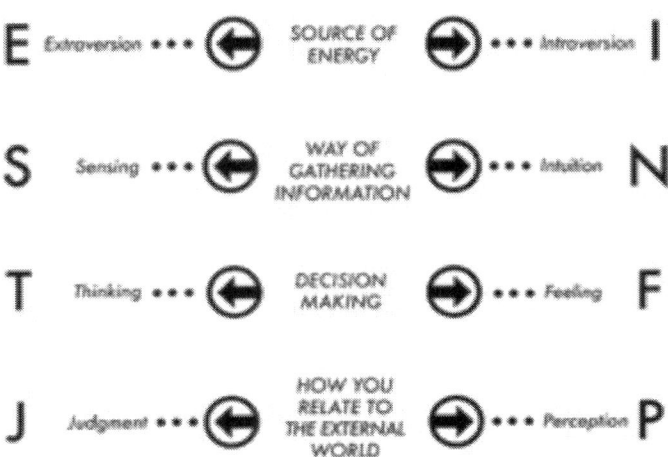

Do you prefer working with others, or primarily by yourself?

When given information do you want details or a general overview.

Do you make decisions based on logic or values?

After making a decision do you act quickly or continue to gather information up to your deadline?

Innate preferences are often hard to identify. The MBTI can indicate differences that may go unnoticed and where an individual may be operating inside or outside of their preferences.

The main drawback to the MBTI is it can be overwhelming and difficult to understand without feedback and validation by a certified consultant. Personality profile results must be observed and discussed to confirm if a person's beliefs or behavior align with their results. With sixteen different personality types, and varying degrees by which each individual may operate within those types, it is important to confirm your results. This is a fault in most MBTI training. A consultant gives a three-hour presentation, loads your head full of information and leaves you with little to no tools for implementing what you have learned. Within a week, much of that information is forgotten and you are back to being stressed out, frustrated, judgmental and unhappy.

Keirsey Temperament Sorter

The Keirsey Temperament Sorter utilizes the sixteen personalities identified in the Myers-Briggs assessment, but breaks them down into four temperaments types; Artisan, Guardian, Idealist, and Rational. Educational Psychologist, David Keirsey, began his work by developing a system to train and coach consultants working with educators and psychologists. Keirsey describes temperament as "a configuration of observable personality traits," such as communication, habits, values, attitudes and talent, and categorizes the four distinct temperaments based on the interaction between human communication (our words) and actions (our deeds).

The 16 Strategies Assessment

While the Keirsey system is widely used across the globe, it can be quite a bit of information to process. I wanted a way to combine the knowledge I had gained from these three personality assessment systems, and the one hundred plus self-help books I had read, into an easily understood and useful guide to help my team understand each other and find sales strategies that best aligned with their individual, innate preferences.

We looked for an assessment that was accurate and easy to understand so salespeople, leaders and teams could implement the information and start seeing results right away. Even with countless personality assessments available, we have yet to find one uniquely geared toward sales. Therefore, we created our own assessment, based on the MBTI, and compiled the best strategies and sales techniques, along with a short description, for each personality type.

We believe when you see the major impact an awareness of your innate preferences can have on your life, you will be excited to learn more. Since our assessment is based on the MBTI, you are able to expand your knowledge through other MBTI books about relationships, leadership, education and parenting. We hope this book will be a springboard into a world of awareness and understanding in all areas of your life.

Our expectation is not that you, as a salesperson, only perform the one strategy assigned by your results. We suggest considering that one strategy as your "Pillar Strategy." Based on Gary Vaynerchuk's concept of "pillar content," your results will become the strategy that all your other efforts funnel into. For example, if your Pillar Strategy is social events, then your newsletter, email campaign and calls should center around inviting customers to your events. Your strategy suggests the solution is to get clients in front of you, frequently. Even though data management, like newsletters and email lists, may take you outside of your comfort zone, they can funnel into your Pillar Strategy and focus on social activities.

Funneling activities that are not naturally among your strongest strengths will increase your productivity and help you reach your goals.

The Importance of Validation

Intelligence, capability, work-ethic and motivation are not typically identifiable through personality assessments and, for most organizations, you will need to observe the person in action to determine these traits. Another limitation of all personality assessments, including DiSC, MBTI, Keirsey— and even our 16 Strategies Assessment, is the use of language for gaining an understanding of each subject's view of their own behaviors or beliefs. Since the use of words and definitions can differ from region, culture and dialect, it is possible for questions to be interpreted differently, so there can be no guarantee of complete accuracy. This is why we recommend validation by a certified consultant. A consultant asks each subject more specific questions about making decisions or gathering and utilizing information to determine if their assessment is accurate. This offers greater context to each question and can clarify individual preference results.

CHAPTER 7
The Assessment

When I took my first personality assessment, I was a little put off by the idea that an assessment could tell me who I was or how I thought. But, I was shocked to find out how accurate the results could be. The assessment is not reading your mind, but it is not taking a blind guess either. Each answer you select helps determine your results, so you are actually telling the assessment what best represents your personality. Remember the phrase, "garbage in, garbage out." If you don't give it your full attention or don't take the assessment seriously, the results will be inaccurate.

The 16 Strategies Assessment consists of multiple-choice questions. Think about who you are on the inside, the authentic you, when you are not being influenced by work or who you become when you need to be to impress others. You will choose the answer that best describes you. There are no correct answers, and there is no type more desirable than another. All types are created equal. Remember, this is intended to create an honest reflection of how you respond in given situations and will help you to understand what you need, and what you already have, on your own journey toward the success you wish to achieve.

Please allow 20 minutes to complete the assessment. Once completed you will immediately receive your results.

Go to www.16strategies.com to take your assessment.

From your camera hover over QR Code and it will take you to the page.

Use the code: U6T8B3P

STOP HERE and Take the Assessment

Continue after you have taken the Assessment...

CHAPTER 8
Reviewing the Results and Strategy

Step 1. Review your results and strategy.

Take some time to read about what strengths, weaknesses and possible blind spots most closely relate to your personality type. Does it sound like you? Can you relate to what the description is saying? If your results seem completely off, think about who you are at the core. Do your answers reflect this? Isabel Briggs Myers said it best;

> *"If you don't [receive accurate results], the problem lies not with the indicator, but with you. Maybe you were in a "work mindset" when you answered the questions...or you had become unusually adept at "veiling your preferences" to suit the wants and needs of your husband or wife, your co-workers, your children. Whatever the case may be, somehow you were inhibited from answering the questions as your 'shoes off self.'"*

If this is true in your case, we suggest you go back and retake the assessment.

The purpose of this book is to give you, the salesperson, the best 'pillar strategy'. Each of our 16 personalities have been analyzed to insure the corresponding strategy will complement the individual personality traits.

Step 2. Review other similar strategies.
Each personality type shares similar preferences with other personality types. To address this, we have listed similar strategies at the bottom of each Result. Please take the time to review each Personality Type and Sales Strategy similar to your own.

Step 3. Edit your results.
Review your Personality Type using a pen and a highlighter. Use the pen to cross through any trait, value or description that you feel does NOT reflect who you are. Use the highlighter to highlight each trait, value and description that DOES reflect who you are. Do this for your similar strategies, as well.

Step 4. You are who you say you are!
This book is here to guide you, not paint you into a corner. As you read each of the Personality Types and Strategies you may find that one of your similar Personality Type or Strategies seem to

fit you better than the Personality Type the Assessment suggested. This is okay. You have my permission to select your own Personality Type and Strategy! You can also select portions of other Personality Type and Strategies to find the best solution for you.

Below is a list of definitions and terms that may help you better understand how to find the best fit for your personality.

Preference
The use of the term Preference throughout this book is intentional. Preference refers to your innate preferences, the traits that are encoded from birth. To be "In Preference" means your beliefs and actions operate in alignment with your innate preferences. Preference also means behaviors that are most natural to you. However, Preference does not pigeon-hole you into only behaving one specific way. It is common to hear "I am an Introvert," as if it is something we can possess. If we think of personality type as a possession, we tend to lock ourselves into a fixed mindset which can lead to an unwillingness to be flexible or to consider a different approach. When we say, "I have a preference for Introversion," it suggests that it is something we prefer, but also acknowledges that we all have the ability to flex to other preferences situationally.

Out-of-Preference

Out-of-Preference refers to a misalignment between your innate preference and your beliefs or actions. There are a few reasons you may be Out-of-Preference from your innate behavior. The most common is because your environment rewards or validates you for thinking or behaving in opposition of your innate behavior. Companies that reward Dominant personality types is one example. If you work for this company but Dominance is not your personality type, you may operate outside of your preferred preference by modeling Dominant traits in order to fit in or keep the job. When this occurs, you may act in a way that causes internal conflict or indecision. But remember, this does not automatically mean the job is not right for you.

Jessica's assessment showed she had a preference for empathy and connection, which she found hard to believe. Jessica had worked as an Attorney for ten years, a job where logic and execution are everything. When I validated Jessica, she told me of her desire to offer low to no cost counsel to residents at the local women's shelter and described her creative hobby of sculpting. Jessica was a playful and creative child. Her parents both shared a preference for logical analysis. Jessica grew up in a structured, but loving household. Jessica trusted her parents career advice when she was ready to head off to college and she was among the top of her class in law school. Jessica's true preference was for empathy and connection, but her childhood and working environment rewarded a preference of logic over empathy. She was operating Out-of-Preference.

If you are working Out-of-Preference but desire the job you have, you may just need to consider a different approach, such as the Pillar Sales Strategy, or work with your secondary results to get closer to your preferred preferences. Jessica was a successful attorney, but her desire to help women at the shelter spoke to her preference for connection and helping others. By offering low-to-no-cost counsel, Jessica had found a way to mold her Out-of-Preference career into an In-Preference situation.

If you feel your assessment is not accurate, you may be Out-of-Preference in some areas of your life. A validation by one of our certified consultants can help you gain a better understanding of your individual personality type.

Flexing
Flexing is the ability and willingness to adapt your preference as needed in certain situations. When asked to review the budget, Jim responded by saying he was not good with numbers. This isn't to say that he does not have the ability to review the budget, Jim has a degree in English and simply prefers words over numbers. When asked to "Flex" his preference toward

avoiding math in order to validate the budget, Jim agreed. Flexing is stepping outside your comfort zone for short periods of time to accommodate a specific situation, person or group.

Strengths

Your strengths are like your superpower. They can be so natural you might not even be aware you have a unique strength that others may not have. Focusing on your natural abilities will make you happier. When you are happier you will participate more often. When you participate more often, you will improve and be more successful.

Weaknesses

These are areas where you naturally perform poorly, struggle to be productive, you may feel completely incompetent. If you have a preference for big picture ideas and creativity, you are likely not gifted at managing details and balancing the books. We all desire to look good and admitting we are vulnerable is uncomfortable. But, if we are honest about our weaknesses, we can find support from others who are willing to help in areas where we fall behind.

Communicating your strengths and weaknesses with others and agreeing to share responsibilities according to each person's natural abilities will increase productivity. This will help you achieve your full potential in areas you might otherwise find difficult, and decrease any stress you may be experiencing in your job.

Blind Spots

These are beliefs and behaviors that are completely outside of our current awareness. It is similar to someone that is color blind. The fact that someone cannot see the color green does not mean the color green does not exist. Being diligent in observing our behaviors and beliefs, and accepting honest feedback, helps us uncover blind spots that may be keeping us from being productive or successful.

James was a committed employee but he had a tendency to talk over people and dismiss their opinions. James was willing to have an honest conversation with me regarding his observed lack of empathy and compassion. James was completely unaware how he made others feel. It wasn't that he didn't care, in fact, he cared deeply, his personality type was just headstrong when it came to getting work done. Since his lack of empathy was outside of his awareness, James didn't recognize when he was coming across as critical. I was able to coach James and we agreed on a signal I could use when he needed to pause and think about how his coworkers might perceive his words or actions. When James responded harshly, I gave him the signal and he would pause, then restate his response to be empathetic. Because he was willing to admit his weakness and create a solution, James became one of the most caring, and cared for, employees in the entire company.

Introversion vs Shyness

One of the most common misconceptions is seeing introversion as shyness. According to the MBTI, introversion is an innate preference that relates to one's area of focus or where they gain energy. An introvert gains energy through reflection or working alone rather than through large groups and parties. On the other hand, shyness is a hesitancy or fear that is based more in experiential or generational beliefs. Introverts can sometimes be mistaken for insecure. The truth is, introverts can be confident and outspoken just as extroverts can be insecure and shy.

Validation

For those of you who would like to have a deeper understanding of your preference or you may feel the results are close to how you see yourself but not completely accurate. We suggest doing a Myers-Briggs Assessment and then have it validated by a certified consultant. A professional validation digs deeper into understanding your given results. You may just want a professional evaluation to ensure that you are as clear as possible to your innate preferences.

Tony's assessment showed a preference for logic over compassion when making decisions. Tony believed this was inaccurate because he always put the needs of his employees and customers first. During his validation, I asked Tony about specific difficult decisions he might make regarding his business. His responses were based in logic. I explained that this didn't mean he wasn't compassionate, but when it came to important decisions, he used logic to determine his actions.

This is a typical pattern of someone with a preference for logic over compassion when making decisions.

Tony mentioned that he often struggles with difficult decisions. He was conflicted by his preference for logic and his need to keep people happy. I explained that focusing on his natural gift for logic, and trusting his decisions, would likely produce better results within his company. Communicating with his employees about the use of logic in making difficult decisions freed Tony from worrying about letting his employees down. It also helped the employees see that Tony's decisions were not personal and were often unavoidable.

Reflection

What is the main thing you took away from your Personality Type and Sales Strategy?

Did your Results identify Strengths you were not aware of?

Did you identify blind spots?

What are you going to change or add to your Sales Strategy, today?

CHAPTER 9
Awareness, Feedback, and Accountability

As obvious as this all seems, I am still amazed at how unaware we can be of our habits, behaviors and decisions. The most important aspect of making lasting change is self-awareness. Now that we are aware of our innate preferences, we can begin to observe how exactly they are impacting our lives, how they cause us to repeat patterns and how they may be preventing us from achieving success. This new self-awareness will keep you from falling back into unconscious, habitual patterns.

The best tools to increase awareness are journaling and tracking. Journaling creates records of our observations of thoughts, beliefs and decisions, much like the food journal I was asked to make by my nutritionist. I suggest keeping a small, hand-held journal with you at all times or using the note section on your phone. When a unempowering thought or belief arises, take a moment to jot it down, as well as any circumstances surrounding it at the time. Return to your notes later and change any discouraging thoughts or beliefs into empowering statements.

You arrive at work and you think to yourself: "I am so stressed out." You take a moment to jot it down in your journal. Later that night, you rewrite the thought to say: "I am strong, powerful and an asset to my team." The next time you think to yourself, "I am so stressed out," you quickly restate the new thought, "I am strong, powerful and an asset to my team." Overtime, this process of acknowledging the thought and restating it, replaces self-deprecating thoughts with positive thinking to encourage and increase happiness.

Tracking is another powerful tool that can guide you toward improvement. Tracking differs from journaling in that you record specific information deemed necessary to achieve desired results. If you wish to lose weight, you need to track what you eat and be aware of calorie intake vs calories burned through activity. If you set a goal, you must track the benchmarks set to get you there. If you want to improve in sales, you must track all your activities.

It is possible to make changes in your life through self-awareness and self-correction, but to make significant changes you need to be open to external feedback. Feedback from a supervisor is effective if the relationship is based on honesty and trust. If the expectations are set too high, it is easy to feel defeated. If expectations are set low, you may feel unvalued or that you are not being taken seriously. Honesty and trust will allow for open conversations about expectations for both you and how you wish to

be held accountable.

Coaching offers the highest form of feedback and accountability. In real estate sales, a coach is paid to check your numbers, actions, appointments, presentations and contracts. Since they are paid for accountability, you can trust them to provide feedback when expectations are not being met. A coach can also review your journal and help reframe any thoughts and beliefs that only serve to clutter up your thinking.

Reflection

What changes would you like to make in your life and career?

What system would you choose to gain greater awareness (feedback, accountability— or both) to make sure your changes stick?

On a scale of 1-10, how committed are you to make these changes?

CHAPTER 10
Working with Other Types

Knowledge of personality types and assessment can be misused if we believed we have the ability to assess others simply by observing them. Situationally, we all have the ability to identify if someone is acting extroverted versus introverted or dominant versus reclusive, but that doesn't speak to what is going on inside their mind. What rules govern how they play the game of life? Are those rules similar to yours? Do they impact the way they make decisions? These are things that cannot be observed.

I have given over a thousand MBTI assessments and have personally validated hundreds of people in my career and I still cannot accurately identify someone's preferences based on observation alone. This is because two people can respond similarly to a situation, but for very different reasons.

It was announced in a quarterly meeting that the company would be changing their Point-of-Sale and Inventory software provider. Immediately, both Patrick and Joanne began aggressively pushing back on the change. They dug their heels in threatened to quit if the change was implemented. Through observation we can assume they were both angry about the software change. However, only Patrick was reacting to the announcement. He had worked on the supply side for over a decade and was integral in forming a partnership with the current software provider. He had also overseen the implementation and training for the software. Patrick argued, "If it works fine, why change it?"

Joanne was the top salesperson for the company. When her arguments were rejected, she stormed out of the room. Later, when asked why she was so angry over changing the software provider she replied, "I don't care about the software, I just don't know why nobody asked what I thought."

Both Joanne and Patrick showed a similar response, but the *reason* for each response was very different. Patrick, an Analyst, prefers the status quo, while Joanne, a General, wants to be seen as part of the decision-making process. For these reasons, it is not effective to respond to Patrick and Joanne the same way. To gain influence, we need to respond to each individual based on their preference. To Patrick we could say, "Change is difficult and at times, not necessary. But in this case, it is necessary to stay ahead of our competitors and be more efficient in the future." To Joanne, we can apologize for not realizing her interest in researching new Point of Sale Software and suggest her involvement in committee meetings if she wishes to be a part of these types of projects. This would likely turn Joanne away, due to her preference for independence, but she would feel validated by your acknowledgement of her ability to participate in these types of decisions.

The best practice when working with others is to train yourself to stay away from judgment. This can be a nearly impossible because the human brain is a matching machine. Sitting on top of your brain stem is a small gland called the Reticular Activating System, or RAS. The function of this gland is to release dopamine into the body when your mind finds or matches something it is looking for. Your brain is literally rewarded for matching. Just think about how powerful this function is for our survival. We have the ability to sort billions of particles of information in seconds because of this simple little gland.

The RAS is what leads us to want to match people and situations together. This, combined with our desire to have certainty and security, causes our brains to categorize people. Have you ever met someone you didn't like at first, then later they became one of your dearest friends? When you first met, your brain matched them to another person or situation that did not give you good feelings. Over time, through new interactions your brain no longer associated them with the previous experience. The desire to match people and experiences is hardwired. We must learn not to associate people with others and allow them to show us who they truly are.

The key to removing ourselves from judgment is to remind ourselves that mother nature, the creator, the universe designed each of us to have individual preferences for the survival of our species. A tribe cannot survive with all hunters and no one to care for the young. Likewise, the same tribe cannot survive with all babysitters and no one gathering food. A society cannot survive without laws and creativity cannot happen without breaking some eggs. It is all part of a bigger picture.

When we are frustrated by others, it is often because the person is not feeling, thinking or acting the way *we* believe *they* should. We get upset when people do not respond the way we respond in a given situation. When driving, when do you get the most frustrated? When someone is not driving the way you wish they were at that moment? If you are in a hurry, you want them to drive faster or get out of your way. But when we are not in a rush, we get frustrated when they insist on getting around us. Our frustration is completely based on our perspective in that given moment.

It can be even more frustrating when the person is a co-worker or employee. You need their participation or buy-in to achieve your goal but they are not acting or responding the way you wish them to act, how you need them to act, or how you would act.

When someone reacts differently than we would in the same situation, we get stressed. This leads to arguments, resentment and eventually, isolation. When we understand that we each have a unique pre-wired view of the world, one that is uniquely and intentionally designed, we can let go of the need to try and convince others to think or act the way we do, we can accept their own innate behaviors.

The first step to resolving your frustration with a co-worker or customer, is to set a meeting to discuss your innate preferences. Be open and honest about what you believe your strengths are, where your weaknesses lie and where you may have blind spots. Allow them to share what they see as their strengths and weaknesses. Do not tell them what you believe about them, find common ground in a goal you both feel is important. Come to the agreement that, despite your innate preferences, you share allegiance to the same goal. This will help you work together successfully. If they are unaware of their innate behaviors offer to have them take the assessment and revisit the conversation.

By letting go of trying to change people's preferences, we listen to their perspective, their opinions and their unique view of the world. Listening creates trust. When they trust you genuinely care about their perspective, they will listen to your perspective in return. My journey to have a better understanding of others stemmed from a deep personal desire to become more influential. Since the beginning of my journey I have had the pleasure to interview, train and coach thousands of salespeople in the real estate and mortgage industries. Influence comes from connection, connection comes from understanding their perspective without judgement. Simply said, the key to being influential is learning to listen without judgment. This does not only mean when you first make the sale or when you first hire someone, this is for your entire relationship.

Reflection

In what situations do you get the most frustrated by others?

How is their unique perspective important to the overall big picture, objective or society as a whole?

How can you handle it the next time someone frustrates you?

CHAPTER 11
Interactions Between Types

If you want to convey a message or belief, or to get your point across, it is your responsibility to communicate clearly to ensure the person you are communicating with understands what you are trying to say. Let's say you are selling equipment enhanced with the latest technology. If you have a preference for the Big Picture but the person you are speaking with prefers Details and Facts, you will need to narrow your explanation of the features and benefits that will help them succeed in a changing marketplace. They are going to look at the equipment and ask how it may improve their current needs. To communicate to them you will need to Flex to their preference for Detail and Facts. Ask them what their current issues are, talk to them about how the new equipment will help them solve their current problems and how the new features will outlast their existing equipment.

When we see things from different perspectives, conflicts are bound to arise. Tyler is one of your best customers. He asks you to move his order to the head of the line because he missed his deadline. Your company's policy is that all orders be treated first-in, first-out. Moving Tyler's order to the front of the line not only breaks company rules, it will delay other customer orders, as well. There are very few orders today and the delay would likely postpone the other orders by just a few minutes. Tyler knows you have the authority to move his order up. He also knows your company's policy. You don't want to lose Tyler as a customer, but you are put off by the arrogance in asking you to break the rules and delay other people's orders. Depending on your personality type you may decide it would be okay to help Tyler, or you may have complete disdain for him.

Let's dig deeper into why you may feel this way.

We divided the 16 personality types into four quadrants based on the dominant personality trait: **Theoretical**, **Inspirational**, **Practical** and **Sympathetic**.

```
                      Big Picture

        ┌─────────────────┬─────────────────┐
        │  Theoretical    │  Inspirational  │
        │                 │                 │
        │  Logical        │  Friendly       │
        │  Ingenious      │  Insightful     │
        │  Theoretical    │  Warm           │
        │  Innovative     │  Possibilities  │
Logical │  Objective      │  Understanding  │ Empathetic
        ├─────────────────┼─────────────────┤
        │  Practical      │  Sympathetic    │
        │                 │                 │
        │  Rules          │  Traditional    │
        │  Facts          │  Values         │
        │  Matter of Fact │  Warm           │
        │  Objective      │  Conscientious  │
        │  Technical      │  Loyal          │
        └─────────────────┴─────────────────┘

                        Detail
```

Further, we listed keywords under each dominant personality trait. These are the beliefs and values by which the four personality types in each quadrant live:

The **Theoretical** quadrant ideals are logical, ingenious and objective. They trust theories and praise innovation.

The **Inspirational** quadrant values friendship, possibilities and being warm, insightful and understanding.

The **Practical** quadrant are matter-of-fact, objective, technical and comfortable with rules and facts.

The **Sympathetic** quadrant is conscientious, warm, loyal and traditional. They place emphasis on values.

	Big Picture			
Logical	Strategist	Debater	Advisor	Guide
	Theoretical		**Inspirational**	
	General	Entrepreneur	Diplomat	Visionary
	Analyst	Operative	Guardian	Designer
	Practical		**Sympathetic**	
	Authority	Contributor	Advocate	Influencer
	Detail			Empathetic

Some of the 16 personality styles share similar beliefs. Think of them as siblings, where they have similar values but present them differently. Along the top of the chart, people with Theoretical and Inspirational personalities are interested in **Big Picture** concepts and ideas. While on the bottom, people with Practical and Sympathetic personalities focus on **Detail** and traditions.

Logical vs Empathetic in Decision Making

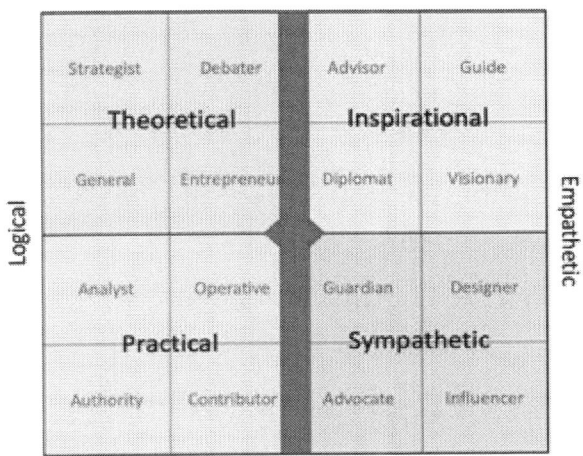

The divider represents the comparison of the two sides, **Logical** vs **Empathetic**. On the left, the Theoretical and Practical personalities will use **Logical** analysis to make their decisions. To achieve their goals, their plan will rely more on technology, process and systems and less on depend less people.

Inspirational and Sympathetic personalities are **Empathetic** and seek compassion first in their decisions. They care deeply about making an impact on others or acting for the good of the world. Achieving their goals will include people in the solution, either by inspiring people, working with people or supporting people. For Empathetic types, the more people they can help, the better.

As you can imagine, this is a common area of conflict. The Logical types wish for efficiency while the Empathetic seek harmony. To bring this into a sales situation, let's say, you are someone with the preference for empathy, which means you value relationships and understanding.

When negotiating a price for the widgets you are selling, you explain they are priced in consideration of the quality and professional staff that your company's reputation was built on. The customer interrupts you abruptly and says, "I don't care about your employees, I just want the lowest price!" If you have experienced this, how did it make you feel? If you haven't, how do you think you would react?

The common misunderstanding is that someone who has a preference for objective decision making doesn't care about people. This couldn't be farther from the truth. They actually care deeply for people, they just don't think about the impact on other people's feelings *initially*. The opposite is also true. Someone with the preference for empathy can be quite logical, it is just not in their nature to base decisions on a logical analysis first.

What personality type are you, **Logical** or **Empathetic**?

List three people you believe use Logic first in their decisions.
    1.
    2.
    3.

In what ways do you align with them?

In what ways do you find conflict?

List three people you believe use Empathy first in their decisions.
    1.
    2.
    3.

In what ways do you align with them?

In what ways do you find conflict?

Big Picture vs Detail in Communication

Big Picture

Strategist	Debater	Advisor	Guide
Theoretical		**Inspirational**	
General	Entrepreneur	Diplomat	Visionary
Analyst	Operative	Guardian	Designer
Practical		**Sympathetic**	
Authority	Contributor	Advocate	Influencer

Facts and Traditions

The most common difference is the way we communicate and gather information. In this graph we look at the differences between people with a preference for **Big Picture** verses people that prefer **Detail.** On the top of the graph, Theoretical and Inspirational personalities will speak in terms of the big picture ideas and concepts. On the bottom, Practical and Sympathetic personalities focus on the tangible facts and details.

Big Picture personalities trust theoretical ideas, possibilities and insights. Someone with a preference for the Big Picture may "trust their gut," or follow their intuition.

People who prefer Detail, look for evidence they can claim as true. This can include rules, laws and traditions, including religious and moral traditions. People with this preference may say "I'll believe it when I see it?" or "the past is the best indicator of the future."

Conflict between these two personality types arises mainly in areas of communication. A preference for the Big Picture speaks in terms of ideas. They move fluidly from one idea to the next, contemplating multiple possibilities at the same time. This can become frustrating to those with a preference for Detail. They prefer to investigate ideas and reflect on their personal experiences. Jumping from one idea to the next feels overwhelming and risky. Detail types can look "stuck in the weeds" to Big Picture types. Their need for concrete plans and specific details drains the excitement out of all the possibilities the Big Picture personality desires.

What personality type are you, **Big Picture** or **Detail**?

Have you ever had to explain a process to someone, like how to get to the airport? Did they get frustrated because you were not being specific enough, or because you gave too much detail?

List three people you believe prefer the Big Picture.

1.
2.
3.

In what ways do you align with them?

In what ways do you find conflict?

List three people you believe prefer Detail.
1.
2.
3.

In what ways do you align with them?

In what ways do you find conflict?

Opposites, Attraction and Conversion

Some of the greatest attractions and conflicts come from our opposing personality types. It is said that deep in our internal programming we are unconsciously aware that we have weaknesses and blind spots. Because of this, we are attracted to people with opposite qualities. This is to protect our lineage, to insure our DNA is passed on for generations. If we are Logical in nature, we are likely good at acquiring assets and not wasting them on impractical opportunities. If we attract a mate with the same qualities, we could raise children together, but the family may lack a warm and nurturing environment. Therefore, our unconscious mind leads us to attract a mate that has the opposite qualities of Empathy, to help pull your head out of the details for a few hours each week and create a nurturing, family environment.

The challenge in most relationships is that we are attracted to people with opposing personalities who we marry, and then spend the rest of our lives trying to make them to see the world the way we do. Or is that just me?

The opposite is true in business. We need employees with strengths that are different from ours but, more often than not, we hire people with similar qualities to our own. Why? Because during the interview process our own personal preferences override the need for different strengths. This is how we end up with blind spots in our business.

On the other hand, we may hire a great candidate with different strengths and then spend time trying to make them think and act according to our own preferences. Or, we may avoid training and development because we just don't enjoy working with them. Either way, we end up with unhappy, underdeveloped employees who could have been outstanding if we spent time working with their natural gifts rather than emphasizing our own.

Ultimately, we need to surround ourselves with complementary personality types rather than mirror images of ourselves and focus on communicating our perspective without pushing people to hold the same beliefs we do. Remember that this is all by design to insure our survival, as well as the survival of our business.

Reflection

When have you found yourself trying to convert someone to your perspective?

How could other personality types benefit you and your organization?

CHAPTER 12
16 Strategies in Teams or Business

Wouldn't it be easier if we all just saw the world the same way? What if we just surrounded ourselves with people who have our same personality type? Unfortunately, this thinking is one of the main reasons businesses fail. An Entrepreneur, Big Picture personality type, whose mind jumps from idea to idea, will find instant kinship with another Entrepreneur, Big Picture personality. They both come up with endless ideas, solutions and possibilities and might decide to form a partnership believing they can change the world. Ninety days in they have spent a lot of time talking, but realize they haven't actually accomplished anything. If they get along so well, why are they not productive?

Plato surmised that just as colonies, such as bees and ants, rely on encoded preferences to ensure each colony functions properly for the survival of their species, the human species likely functions with the same encoded preferences. If we all had the internal desire to lead people who would follow us? If we all had the need for consistency and security who would innovate to ensure our survival? If we all valued logical decisions over compassion and empathy, how would we treat each other? Would we even desire that world?

Business is no different than a colony. Different personalities are needed for the success and survival of the business. When a business is in the start-up phase there is a large need for Theoretical ideas and Inspirational motivation. When the business moves to stability, needs will shift from innovation to the process, systems and accountability preferred by Sympathetic and Practical types. Mature businesses exist in all phases simultaneously, meaning they are growing sales, providing consistent quality products and services, and innovating to stay relevant. A business is not sustainable without the strengths of various personality types.

Motivational speaker and sales guru, Jim Rohn, once asked why some salespeople produce little, some produce mediocre and some excel. He said he was determined to convince his low producers to become top producers, "even if it kills me." He added, "I almost died!"

His point was to say we should focus on the top producers and stop trying to motivate the middle and low producers. This sounds logical, but if we study the unique characteristics of each person as an individual, we find there is more to being a top producer than simply motivation. To this day, I regret what little time I gave the lower producers I once led as they are now some of the most successful top producers. They simply needed more time to find the strategy that worked best for their personality type. As you may guess, many of them left my company because I didn't give them the attention and leadership they deserved.

Hiring Trends

I have worked with sales managers, team leaders and branch managers all tasked with leading and training a sales team. I mentioned before how many sales organizations try to identify specific qualities or personality types to shortcut the cycle of hiring and training new salespeople. This tactic will almost always fail for the following reasons:

Hiring the Michael Jordan of Sales

When you are leading a sales team in a highly competitive industry, you may not have the financial resources to hire the "M.J." of the sales world. Worse yet, is when you have the "M.J." of sales, everyone else will offer them incentives to come to their company. This makes it increasingly difficult to keep your "M.J's" comp plan competitive while maintaining your profitability.

Hiring "Like Me"

So, why not just hire a team of independent, driven, self-motivated salespeople, just like you? Because independent, driven, self-motivated people like you start their own companies and become your competitor within two to three years, and often take your people with them. This is damaging to the long-term success of your organization and puts you in a never-ending cycle of hiring.

Hiring the "A" Type

The use of personality assessments to narrow candidates and select a specific type of personality for sales positions is not new. It is a common belief that there is a specific personality type which is more driven, easier to train or more personable at making sales.

There are two challenges with this strategy. The first is, many interviewees are already keen to what answers they should choose in order to get a favorable result on an assessment used for hiring salespeople. In fact, you wrote the qualities you are looking for in your ad. Instead of being honest about their true preferences they "cheat" the assessment. You get the pleasure of discovering their true preferences thirty days after they were hired, leaving you with the challenge of coaching someone with training developed for another personality type, or terminating them and going back to the drawing board.

The second, you will miss out on some of the best people. People that will support you and grow your business, with outstanding results. All businesses rely on different personality types to maintain customer satisfaction and to stay relevant. If all your salespeople are one personality type, your business will either struggle to maintain a good customer base or struggle to innovate based on the customer's needs. A good business needs to do both.

An organization I previously was involved with used an internal personality profile to determine what personality type would be most effective in their sales manager positions. The type of person they were seeking was someone that was driven, had a need for approval, was loyal and followed the rules. When I tested for the position, my assessment showed I was highly driven and had a need for approval, but I was also stubborn and entrepreneurial. Despite the lack of congruency, the business owner, Brian, took a chance on me. Fortunately, Brian had a clear understanding of personality assessments. We were able to discuss how he could manage my stubbornness and entrepreneurial drive. Best of all, we agreed to a three-year commitment. This gave him the security of knowing he could rely on me for a certain period of time and kept me from feeling trapped in a long-term position.

Brian purchased a failing real estate brokerage in the middle of the 2009 recession. The traditional success path for a brokerage is to recruit top producing agents from other companies. During the recession, many top producing agents were also struggling to find effective ways to generate business. Many were also unwilling to learn new techniques.

To save the company, I had to innovate and come up with a new strategy. Unemployment was high and the members of the existing agent pool were stuck in their old ways. We created an internal real estate school to hire and train displaced workers looking for a career change, train new agents by helping them sell their first home and added new sales techniques that were effective in our local market. In just two years we went from a nearly bankrupt brokerage to one of the top ten out of 700 offices in the nation. It was so successful Brian quickly adopted the strategy into his four other brokerages, allowing them to also out-perform the market during the downturn.

I was not a good fit for Brian's assessment, but I was the right fit for what his newly acquired brokerage needed at that time. If Brian had relied solely on the assessment, he would not have chosen someone with the qualities of innovation from an Entrepreneur personality type. Innovation was exactly what his business needed. Brian found the driven, faithful employee he desired, and I was able to perform at my best without feeling confined by rules and long-term obligations.

If you are leading a sales team or wish to lead a team sometime in the future, you will want to take note of the keys to success in hiring.

Hiring for Success

Hire people connected to the vision, first!
It doesn't matter what the personality type, if someone is not connected to your vision, they won't be successful and, most likely, they won't stay. If they are passionate and connected to the vision, they will become an asset to your organization no matter their personality type. "Where there is a *why*, there is a *way*!"

Always use a personality assessment.
This will allow you open conversations regarding personality traits you have in common, where you differ, where you will align, where you will experience conflict and where you share blind spots. This is an outstanding way to develop rapport. If you have an existing team, I suggest doing an assessment and a

follow up conversation with every one of your employees. Find connections in their values to the mission, vision and values of your company or team.

Ongoing Feedback

"Set It and Forget It" is not a successful strategy in business. You must provide feedback to your team, not only about projects and sales quotas, but also on personality traits that are developing success or creating frustration. Honest feedback, <u>without judgment</u>, will give you and your employees the opportunity to reflect on their personality type and to find solutions without shame for behaving within their internal preferences.

Reflection

In what ways does your organization or business promote and support different personality types?

What is one hiring lesson you will implement?

CHAPTER 13
Increasing Productivity

If you have a team you love but are not satisfied with their overall performance, it is possible to increase productivity by encouraging them work within their preferences. This is possible, but not always easy. One common challenge is that our most consistent, loyal and easy to manage salespeople are often not the most motivated, thick-skinned or goal oriented.

You recently promoted Sarah to sales because she was an outstanding sales support coordinator. Her attention to detail and high standards for customer service equated to loyal, repeat customers. But Sarah's lack of drive and avoidance of conflict resulted in mediocre sales numbers. Of course, the only way to reach your goals is to increase sales, but you fear you might lose loyal customers if you replace Sarah. You are not happy because sales are lacking and Sarah is not happy because she feels she is letting you down. You feel trapped. You both simply avoid the accountability conversations and your business bumps along. Sound familiar? We have all been there.

Instead of letting Sarah go, take time to learn more about her personality type. Sarah's preference is one-on-one time with clients, but she is not comfortable giving presentations or being put in the spotlight. Sarah cares deeply about her client's personal lives, she watches social media, takes time after hours and her own money to deliver gifts and personal messages. Sarah sees her customers as friends. She says she wouldn't want to do her job anymore if she couldn't be friends with her clients. With Sarah's personality, it's no wonder clients feel connected to her and remain loyal. This is what you want for your customers, don't you?

You have been training Sarah for the past year on making cold calls and following up with leads from the website to generate business. She doesn't enjoy this, but she does because wants to keep her job and is loyal to you.

With your new understanding of personality type you ask Sarah, "How do you feel about spending more time with your customers?

Sarah: "I would love that!"

You: "If I approved $100 a month for you to spend on small gifts for your customers, would that help you?"

Sarah: "Of course, what's the catch?"

You: "Do you feel comfortable asking each client to refer you to their friends and colleagues?"

Sarah: "Yes."

You: "Can I count on you to get ten referrals by the end of the month?"

Sarah: "I can do that!"

Do you believe Sarah would respond positively to this type of accountability? Do you believe she would be excited to save some of her own money but spend more time with her clients? Of course, she will. In fact, she felt so empowered she received ten referrals within the first week. Why did this simple change make such a big difference?

In the past, you asked Sarah to generate business outside her preference, which she did out of obligation. Generally, when we do something purely out of obligation, it is hard to generate excitement. Sarah's low energy and disinterest in following up on website leads and making cold calls transferred to her clients and affected her results. Your initial thought was to replace her with a driven, hard charging sales person, but you knew her loyal customers would be unhappy and might follow her to a competitor. By spending a few extra hours with her over a six-week period of time and learning more about preferences, you were able to give her the tools she needed to develop a more effective sales approach. In the end, she felt valued, remained loyal and her productivity continues to increase.

It would be remiss of me not to mention that Sarah may never be the top salesperson. To offset this, you could reduce her territory, which would keep her focus within smaller parameters. You could then either add an additional person to help Sarah, or expand the territory of a top performer. But letting her go, finding a new salesperson, training them and retaining clients is a monumental task filled with pitfalls— and loyalty can be hard to find.

Sales vs Operations

The war between sales and operations erupted long before the Hatfields and McCoys (or Katy Perry and Taylor Swift, for the younger generation.) It is easy to see how these conflicts arise between these two camps. Salespeople are paid mostly on bonuses or commissions while those in operations are paid hourly or are salaried. Salespeople are rewarded for ingenuity and creativity and operations is rewarded for consistency and speed. Salespeople want more and more business and operations want less pressure and stress. And we wonder why they build barriers, retain allies and defend their positions.

The most effective solution I have found for resolving the conflict between operations and sales is to open up the conversation of innate preferences. When you think about it, the operations person was likely selected for their position because they desired a consistent paycheck, a scheduled work week and didn't want to deal with conflict. The salesperson, on the other hand, often prefers flexibility, the ability to earn more if they do more and they accept conflict as an inevitable part of sales.

To manage the monumental task of ending this "100-Year War" between sales and operations we offer a Group Dynamics Workshop. In our Workshop we give each participant, including leadership, an MBTI Assessment, perform a group Validation to confirm accuracy, allow the team to talk about strengths, weaknesses and blind spots, and how different personalities relate to each other. We have found this to be a vital tool for businesses, from small start-ups to large, Fortune 500 organizations. If you are struggling with low performance from your team due to the internal conflict of sales and operations, this may be a solution for you.

When your sales team is connected to the vision of the company, your role is to set and manage expectations within their ability and individual preferences. This will result in a stable, loyal and successful sales team.

Reflection

How can hiring and leading different personality types improve your sales, productivity and profits?

What two things are you going to implement immediately with your team or organization?

    1.

    2.

CHAPTER 14
Closing Thoughts

Your unique beliefs and habits produce the results you are experiencing. Have gained self-awareness you can now make the necessary changes to get the results you desire.

You have learned that conflict comes from our judgement of others and that understanding different personalities is necessary for the survival of our species, as well as our businesses. Releasing judgement will further reduce stress, which will increase happiness in your work and life.

You now have the knowledge to surround yourself with others that do not share the same perspective. Being open to their opinions gives insight into areas you may be overlooking due to your own blind spots. You know to be patient with opposite personality types and to not try to push them to be like you.

If you wish to be more effective with people you must become influential, and influence comes from trust. Build trust by listening and understanding without judgement. This helps you become a more understanding spouse and a more effective leader, coach and sales person.

Next you will read what effective sales strategy is in alignment with your innate preferences (based on the assessment you took in Chapter 8) and sixteen other strategies you can choose from to compliment your pillar strategy. These new sales activities will align with your innate preferences. This will reduce stress and internal conflict, causing you to feel better about sales activities, encouraging you to do more. More actions will equal better performance and better performance will produce better results. You are on your way to success!

No strategy is valuable without implementation. Take the time to write out a specific plan to implement your pillar strategy and secondary strategies that will flow into your pillar strategy. Give yourself realistic timelines for execution, implementation, and results.

Track and measure all your activities and results to ensure you are on track with your goals. Create a feedback loop by journaling and having a supervisor or coach review your activities and results. Remember there is no change without tracking!

At 16 Strategies, we offer a variety of services to help you improve performance and reduce stress. This includes team workshops, sales workshops and coaching. Please feel free to contact us for additional resources to support you and your team.

I started the book saying, "We all desire success, happiness and fulfillment. Isn't that what life is about? Pushing our limits, finding what we love and enjoying the experience along the way?" This book is my way of helping you on that journey.

The following pages are descriptions of each, individual Results and sales strategies that best suit each of the 16 personality types. Remember, you decide who *you* are. Feel free to pick any sales strategies you feel will work best to help you find the success you desire, even if it is for a Result different from the one your were assigned by the assessment. You control your own journey. This information will help make that journey more enjoyable for you, and those around you.

Section Two: 16 Strategies

Personality Types and Sales Strategies

Diplomat	107
Visionary	112
Advisor	117
Guide	124
Strategist	129
Debater	135
General	140
Entrepreneur	146
Authority	153
Contributor	159
Analyst	164
Operative	169
Advocate	175
Influencer	182
Guardian	186
Designer	192
About the Author	198

Diplomat

Traits

Externally Focused: The Diplomat places their external focus on the support of others.

Cooperative: Diplomats are able to build connections among people with diverse opinions. They are loyal followers and can be inspiring leaders.

Big Picture: They are curious and motivated by the possibilities that contribute to the good of people.

Decisive: Once the decision has been made, the Diplomat will take the responsibility and facilitate the organization of others, and move the project to completion.

Values
Cooperation
Loyalty
Honesty
Responsibility

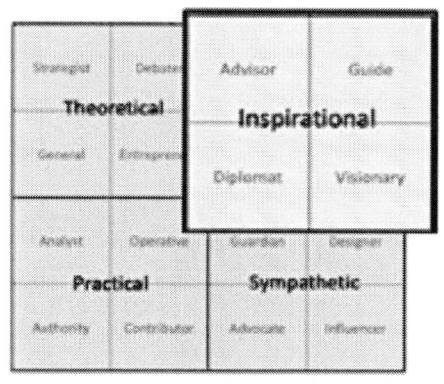

Description

Caring, optimistic and driven, Diplomats attract others with their positive and proactive outlook. They make formidable salespeople with their constant desire to help others and can-do attitude. They are quickly promoted into leadership roles but, over time, they can get stressed by sales quotas and the responsibility of the accountability of others.

Diplomat

Diplomats desire a people-oriented work environment with plenty of work to be done. They will tirelessly finish a project for the simple acknowledgement from their peers or superiors. With a preference for being considerate, they are often the ones creating harmony within a group, mending relationships and taking charge when the situation arises.

Having a higher purpose, such as a charitable contribution, only drives the Diplomat even more, due to their insatiable appetite to impact as many people as possible. When a Diplomat believes that the product or service they sell— either directly, like TOMS shoes, who, for every pair of shoes purchased, sends a pair of shoes to a child in need, one for one, or indirectly, as in "When I make a sale, I will personally donate my time or money to charity"— they become intrinsically motivated.

Conversely, Diplomats can be judgmental of others, at times even harsh. They are equally as hard on themselves and they do not take criticism well. Therefore, they tend to be the most reserved of all extrovert types. They can overthink things, become recluse and withdraw if their ideas are challenged or criticized.

Strengths
    Natural Leader
    Excellent social skills
    Great sense of humor
    Creates harmony
    Considerate

Weakness
    Sensitive to criticism

Diplomat

Judgmental
Tendency toward gossip
Overly talkative

Opportunities

Look for opportunities to get out of the office and spend time talking with your clients and potential customers. Long-term relationships will come naturally, be sure to remember to ask for referrals to grow your sales pipeline. Find a higher purpose to attach to your goals or sales. Donate a portion of your sales to a non-profit that you have or had a personal experience with. A personal mission will drive you far more than the money.

Avoid

You may feel the need to pursue perfection, this will open you to self-analysis and push you into over-thinking and self judgement. Self-judgement will paralyze you and prevent you from achieving your full potential. You have strong values, but this can lead to becoming too judgmental of others. Remember the age-old saying, "If you can't say anything nice, don't say anything at all."

Famous Diplomats
Ben Stiller
Bono
Jennifer Lawrence
Diane Sawyer
Morgan Freeman

Diplomat Sales Strategy

The Diplomat's Strategy must have a positive impact or, if nothing else, be something that cannot negatively hurt humanity.

Diplomat

Selling something you do not believe in is not an option for this personality type.

Find a company or a cause you care deeply about. If you were a foster child or were adopted. You may have a deep emotional connection to children in the foster care system. Ask your company if they would allow you to donate a portion of your time or commission to a non-profit organization that supports foster children. Where there is a will, there is always a way. Don't take no for an answer, find a creative solution, even if it is simply an agreement with yourself. You can promise yourself that each time you make a sale, you will volunteer thirty minutes of your personal time to help the non-profit.

Once you establish your cause begin by sharing your story of why the cause is important to you and why selling the product or service you are selling is making a difference. You must trust that being open and sharing will attract customers that share deep emotional connections to similar causes. This will build trust and opening their mind to listen to your presentation. More importantly it will motivate you to do your best because you are making a difference.

Mike, a Mortgage Broker, who built his business by doing just that. In the news about a local police officer was suspended for donating a car seat to a mother he had pulled over. See at that time, in his city, it was illegal for Police officers to give any money or items of value to citizens. It was seen as a form of bribery.

When the Police officer pulled over the mother with her young daughter in the car the Officer asked her why her daughter was not in a car seat. The mother explained that money was tight, and she had to make the choice between buying food or buying a car seat. The Officer trying to be caring asked the woman to follow her to a nearby Walmart where he purchased her a car seat and sent her on her way.

The mother was so grateful she posted it on social media and the story went viral. This was unfortunate for the Police officer as he had broken the rules and his department had no choice but to suspend him for the violation.

When Mike saw this in the news he was dumbfounded, "How could this be true?" he asked. Mike made it his mission to correct this injustice. Mike formed a 501c3 non-profit organization. The goal of the non-profit was to raise money so Police, Firefighters, and Social Workers could request money for families in need. Mike and his company donated a portion of their earnings from every loan they originated to the non-profit.

They talked openly about their passion for solving this problem. The more they donated the more the word spread about how Mike and his company was caring for their community. Today over 50% of Mike's business comes from First Responders, but better yet Mike and his company are helping hundreds of needy families.

Other Sales Strategies to Consider

The Diplomat shares similar personality traits with the **General, Advisor** and **Visionary**. Take the time to read those Sales Strategies also.

MBTI - ENFJ

Visionary

Traits

Extenal Focus: Visionaries have a strong external focus, searching for opportunities that arise where they can shine.

Innovative: Extremely innovative and resourceful, especially when it comes to connections between people.

Persuasive: Passionate and keenly tuned into the people around them, they quickly attract others that wish to share the excitement the Visionary radiates.

Spontaneous: Part of their allure is their ability to go with the flow. No matter what happens they have the ability to stay positive by finding the one shining star in a dark sky.

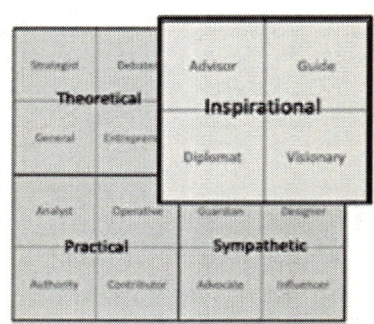

Values
- Adventure
- Connection
- Positivity
- Authenticity

Description

Visionaries see life as a creative adventure full of opportunities. They have the unique ability to see patterns and opportunities that others are completely unaware of. In fact, they spend their spare time dreaming about all the possibilities that life holds.

Visionary

At times, they can frustrate others when they jump from idea to idea and plan to plan. Visionaries cannot help themselves as they have a wide range of interests, positive attitude, and see the world full of possibilities. This makes it difficult for them to make a commitment to one path, since a decision could cut off other amazing possibilities.

Outgoing, energetic, and persuasive Visionaries are natural at sales. Their flexible attitude can pivot quickly to the customers shifting demands. They also have a keen ability to understand people. Some would say they seem to have the ability to anticipate an opponent's next move.

A Visionary's overuse of flattery and compliments can come across as insincere. Other people's admiration is their greatest desire. This can leave them to over promise things or agree to terms that are outside of their control. This leads to disappointment of customer expectations.

Their work environment requires a lot of freedom and flexibility for them to explore all possibilities. Drama between coworkers will disrupt their focus and their desire for harmony gives them the need to settle conflict. Visionaries can become outstanding leaders as long as they are not saddled with long term management of projects or process.

Strengths
    Flexible
    Persuasive
    Enthusiastic
    Outgoing
    Imaginative

Visionary

Weaknesses
> Non-Committal
> Over Enthusiastic
> Over Promises
> Can't handle rejection

Opportunities
Find an organization with strong growth and a lot of opportunities for advancement. This will give you room to grow. Take additional time to flesh-out the "realistic" details of your ideas before sharing them. Make short-term commitments to your employer and coworkers so they can trust that they can rely on you for a period of time.

Avoid
Avoid the overuse of gestures: "85% of our customers return" instead of *"all* of our customers return." People that value detail lose trust in people that overestimate the value of something or its impact. Remember, under promise and over deliver, is the secret to customer happiness.

Famous Visionaries

> Gwen Stephani
> Robert Downey Jr.
> Ellen DeGeneres
> Robin Williams

Visionary Sales Strategy

The key phrase for a Visionary in sales is "Keep them in front of people!" As a natural influencer you cannot help but to share your enthusiasm with other people, this is your Superpower. You have the ability to instinctively identify who in the room is interested in what you are selling and who is not.

Look for opportunities to be in groups of people, either by networking or presenting. Being a presenter or teacher, will allow your natural exuberance to work for you instead of against you. Be sure to take extra time to rehearse to ensure your message is delivered clearly, in a timely manner, and that you stay on topic.

Find an industry topic you care about that directly impacts your customers. Create a 15-30 minute presentation that includes:

What industry threat, concern, or opportunity you are interested in.

How might it affect your customer or industry?

How does your product, service, or company provide a specific and unique solution?

What should the listener do?

Deliver this presentation as frequently and as consistently as you can. Make adjustments to the presentation only to increase the conversion ratios in regards to sales, not your preference to make it unique or to avoid rejection.

Your instincts will suggest you *only* need to follow up with warm leads. We have learned through experience to follow up with

Visionary

ALL leads, not just the people that showed interest, since customer's motivations change every day. Your fortune is in your follow-up.

Ask for help with accountability to your commitment to presentation and your follow up. Systems and CRMs will not be effective accountability for you because, as a Visionary, you are less focused on what needs to be accomplished and more focused on who is paying attention and how you are perceived. This will require you to have weekly accountability with a supervisor or a Coach.

Your outgoing and authentic personality will attract other salespeople wanting to learn from you and your collaborative personality will want to take time to help them. You may even want to create a team to help even more salespeople find success. This is an easy distraction from what needs to get done (lead generation). Managing needy personalities will zap your energy as you try endlessly to fill them up. Be an independent role model, they can follow and emulate, without making any commitments to be responsible for their success. In the end you will find you are more successful and happier.

Other Sales Strategies to consider

The Visionary shares similar personality traits with the **Entrepreneur, Diplomat** and **Guide**. We suggest reviewing those Sales Strategies also.

MBTI: ENFP

Advisor

Traits

    <u>Internal Focus:</u> The Advisor focuses on their intuitive understanding of complex meanings and human relationships.

    <u>Empathic:</u> They have the ability to deeply understand the feelings and personal motivations of people. This allow them to be very influential to others.

    <u>Purpose:</u> Advisors bring meaning and purpose to everything they do, including their work. They look for opportunities to create plans to positively impact people.

    <u>Driven:</u> Their purpose fuels their passion and drive. They are quick to help organize people or a plan to achieve their purpose.

Values
    Morals
    Creativity
    Cooperation
    Relationships
    Unconventional

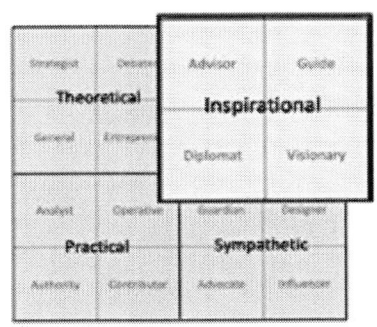

Description
    Kind and caring in nature, Advisors have an intuitive understanding of other people. They are altruistic but not dominant because they lead by example. Rooted in their own personal values they believe by being a good person, others will naturally want to emulate you. The rarest of all personality types, they often feel like

an outsider even though they spend much of their time trying to make others happy at the expense of their own mental peace.

Advisors prefer to work alone in a peaceful environment. They desire respect and appreciation for their contributions. They thrive in areas full of imagination and creativity, yet they are happiest when they have control of their own schedules, responsibilities and projects.

They do not take criticism well because they are their own toughest critics. You cannot be as hard on them as they are on themselves. In a corporate environment, they may find themselves torn between managing tough decisions and their values. They will contemplate all the possible implications of a decision leading them to experience frustration and delay. This can make them look like a procrastinator to others.

Advisors tend to be stubborn to other's opinions that do not align with their current position or plan. Even though, at times, their own ideas may be unrealistic or unachievable. Advisors have a tendency to overlook important facts and have unrealistic standards for themselves and those around them, which can lead to internalized stress when things don't work out the way they had hoped.

Strengths
    Imaginative
    Understanding
    Forgives Easily
    Respectful
    Warm and Friendly

Weaknesses
    Stubborn
    Can be unrealistic.
    Can't take criticism.
    Can overthink things.

Opportunities
    Look for opportunities to share your values through a creative process. Find ways to take your internal thoughts and ideas and share them with your customers and clients. Many Advisors are talented writers. This is an ideal way to share common values. Find connection and common ground with each client individually, understanding that, even if all other values differ, you can always find one thing to focus on that you both desire or care deeply about.

Avoid
    Avoid people, techniques, and strategies that go against your personal values. This will slow you down and deplete your energy. This may include things like selling a product you do not believe in or calling people during family time. Find solutions or mental "work-arounds" that do not violate your ideologies.

Famous Advisors
    Oprah Winfrey
    Lady Gaga
    Martin Luther King Jr.
    Al Pacino

Advisor

Advisor Sales Strategy

First, spend time determining who your ideal client is, not only for the product or service you are selling but also to identify those who share the same values. Begin with your company's mission statement. What attracted you to work there in the first place? How does your company's mission align with your personal beliefs and values? Choose two or three key company values that you can firmly stand behind.

Once you have determined the connection between you and you company's mission, you can find customers who also share your dream. Take a minute and write out what type of customers share your passion. We call them *Dream Keepers*.

Geography: Where do they Live and Work?

Education: What level of Education do they have?

Work: What type of work do they do?

Hobbies: What do they do when not at work?

Interests: What do they think about or read about?

Psychography: What do they believe to be true?

Next, show your customers that you share their same values. Use your creativity to share your dream and develop content that resonates with your customers. Be sure to not lose sight of how your company's mission and how it supports the shared vision.

Advisor

This content is best shared in a blog, vlog (video blog) or a podcast format. The reason we suggest blogs, vlogs and podcasts is because they are what we call "evergreen." Evergreen refers to content that is permanent and searchable in the location where it is hosted. Facebook, Instagram, Twitter, and LinkedIn posts are temporary in nature and are quickly lost in a pool of posts. Evergreen content will show up in searches and can be shared multiple times for years.

This blog, vlog or podcast will be hosted via social sites such as LinkedIn and Facebook. The content can also be shared in monthly newsletters and emails to customers and fellow businesses in the community. It will take discipline and time, but your customers will come to think of you as an expert.

Daniel is not your typical sales person. In fact, you probably wouldn't even know Daniel worked in sales unless you walked into his office. Daniel feels unmotivated and disconnected from his work as an Insurance Agent who specializes in residential and personal property insurance. Daniel loves the mountain community he lives and works in. He especially cares for the peaceful forests surrounding the town. He feels the forests are mistreated and deeply desires his community to work together to preserve them.

The mission statement for the large company he works for is, "To inspire, protect and restore your dreams. Because we believe a dream is the most valuable thing you'll ever own."

Daniel's dream is to protect the forests that surround his community, and to preserve them for the next generation.

He recognizes the connection between his dream and his company's mission. Daniel sees how his own values align with the values of his company. This gives Daniel a passion for his company that he didn't have before.

Daniel writes:

<u>My Dream Keepers</u>
live in my community
work in my community
college graduates
business professionals
earn $80k+
enjoy being outdoors
active
hikers
runners
bicyclists
idealists
nature lovers
own a home
own expensive hobby equipment

Daniel begins blogging about specific mountain trails. He includes detailed descriptions of wildlife, and the natural beauty of their community. Daniel thoughtfully talks about the need for proper management of a fire boundary around your home and how his company can provide personal advice on how to protect investments like homes and expensive hobby equipment with his unique insurance options.

It didn't happen overnight but Daniel became known as the top advisor in his community when it came to protecting the forests for the next generations. He built trust and connection through his Dream Keepers strategy which show his passion and commitment to his community. He also sells a lot of insurance!

Other Sales Strategies to Consider

The Advisor shares similar personality traits with the **Strategist**, **Diplomat**, and **Guide**. We suggest reviewing those Sales Strategies also.

MBTI: INFJ

Guide

Traits

Internal Focus: The Guide's internal focus on their inner core of values is what guides their decisions and interactions.

Intellectual: They are fascinated by the complexities of human personalities and enjoy reading, discussing and reflecting.

Moral: Guides place importance on altruistic values and moral commitments. They value relationships and true connection.

Autonomous: Adaptable and flexible, they prefer to work without the supervision of others.

Values
Caring
Original
Concerned
Valued
Loyal

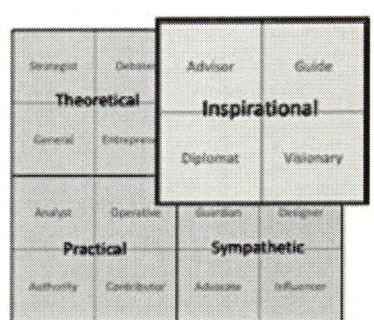

Description

The Guide is loyal and compassionate. Internally driven by their own moral compass, they spend their lives in noble service to society. Volunteering and focusing more on life's meaning with little interest in status or wealth.

They have an idealistic vision for the world and quietly influence others around them to help fulfill this vision. With many projects going and a desire to pursue perfection, Guides often fail to fully complete any one project. Because they are never satisfied with themselves or their work, the projects remain unfinished.

They prefer to work alone or in small groups with people who share their values. To get full buy-in from a Guide, a company's commitments and principals must be in alignment. Guides dislike environments that are highly competitive or people who are more concerned about a paycheck than the purpose.

Guides avoid leading others as they are non-confrontational and unwilling to criticize others, optimistically hoping things will work themselves out. They give the impression they are in agreement by withholding their opinions, only to lash out later over something insignificant.

Strengths
    Loyalty
    Compassion
    Empathy
    Passion
    Positive Outlook

Weaknesses
    Non-confrontational
    Withholds Opinion
    Misses Deadlines
    Too many commitments

Opportunities

Seek purpose-driven organizations, with a vision you can passionately get behind. Attend multiple organizational meetings and events to remain engaged and keeping your passion and focus. Remind yourself that when you miss deadlines other people can be inconvenienced or negatively affected. When possible, work in small groups, make a purposeful effort to complete your part of the project on-time. The accountability to other people will push you to meet deadlines.

Avoid

Avoid high pressure sales environments and companies that are driven by financial performance over people. Avoid isolating yourself from others as this may allow self-doubt to creep in and paralyze your activities. Avoid withholding your opinion, it is important to the group even if you wait until after the meeting and send it in a well thought out email. This will prevent the buildup of emotions that can erupt unexpectedly.

Famous Guides
John Lennon
Princess Diana
Johnny Depp
William Shakespeare

Guide Sales Strategy

Your passion and desire to be of service to your community is your superpower. Make service your calling card, and be the difference in your community by sponsoring a food, clothing or shoe drive. Create an annual schedule and participate throughout the year.

When	What
January	Follow-up call and newsletter w/photos of previous event.
February	Supply drive for the armed forces.
March	Follow-up call and newsletter w/photos of previous event.
April	
May	Volunteer clean-up at local parks.
June	Follow-up call and newsletter w/photos of previous event.
July	
August	School supply drive.
September	Follow-up call and newsletter w/photos of previous event.
October	Winter coat and shoe drive.
November	Follow-up call and newsletter w/photos of previous event.
December	Holiday food drive.

Once you create your schedule promote it on social media, with fliers door-to-door and in your advertising. Get the community, businesses and your customers involved. Your engagement in the community and connection to service will attract others that wish to support you. Step out of your comfort zone and ask for support in helping you with your work goals. Say something like this:

"Thank you for supporting our community food drive. I wouldn't be able to do this without the support of my company (Company Name).

In fact, if you hear of anyone that is in need of (product or service), please let me know. This will allow (Company Name) continue to support me and the needs in our community."

No doubt being this direct will be difficult for you in the beginning. But it is a necessary step if you want your passion for giving back to also provide an income. You will need to learn to get comfortable being uncomfortable and <u>ask for the business</u>.

Other Sales Strategies to consider
The Guide shares similar personality traits with the **Visionary, Advisor,** and **Debater.** We suggest considering those Sales Strategies also.

MBTI: INFP

Strategist

Traits

Internal Focus: The Strategist focuses on global perspective and impact with little regard for current popular opinion or establishment.

Visionary: They have a clear vision of the possibilities that the future holds.

Strategic: Once they have outlined the general structure of their vision, they move quickly to develop a strategy to achieve their goal.

Impersonal: Simply put, "It's not about you... it's about the plan."

Values
Achievement
Original
Competence
Independence
Efficiency

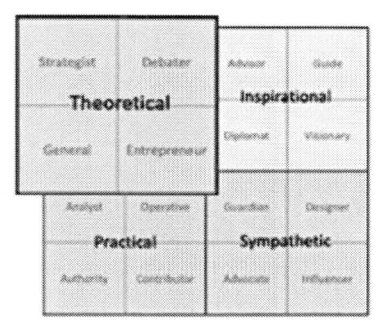

Description

The Strategist is one who sees the direction the world is moving and develops a plan to leverage this by strategically positioning themselves or their company to have a unique advantage. They are insightful, conceptual, and big picture thinkers and can be a unique asset to their company.

Strategist

Strategists are calm, confident, and diligent. They are outstanding students due to their careful preparation and practice. They have a fascination with science and technology that plays a role in any strategy they implement.

They can be overly critical at times. They have little tolerance for routine, or the messiness of human emotions in the workplace. When this occurs, they may become reserved, single-minded and aloof. Don't try to outwit the Strategist, they are always four moves ahead of you.

Strengths
>   Works Independently
>   Persistent
>   problem-solving
>   Critical Thinking
>   Results Driven

Weaknesses
>   Dislikes Routine
>   Single-minded
>   Can Overthink
>   Impatient
>   Cold and Impersonal

Opportunities
Your strength is the ability to see patterns emerging that others do not see. Before approaching senior leadership with your big picture and original ideas, build trust through your actions and performance. Find creative outlets to share your strong views on expected outcomes. Blogging, vlogging or podcasts are great outlets for expressing ideas.

Avoid

You may have the tendency to expect others to see opportunities, possibilities and insights as clearly as you do. Understand this is an ability that is unique to only a few. Avoid getting frustrated or aloof if others don't quickly accept your perspective. Avoid getting into intellectual arguments with your supervisors or co-workers. You may win the argument but will lose respect.

Famous Strategists
  Lance Armstrong
  Katie Couric
  Mark Zuckerburg
  Sir Isaac Newton

Strategist Sales Strategy

A Strategist can do anything they put their mind to. Consistent focus and determination are your superpowers. Your persistence and thick skin will serve you well in sales.

Your strategy is not just to make one sale, but tens, if not hundreds, or thousands. You need to fish in larger ponds to find groups or companies that need a lot of the product or service you are selling. Begin by networking one client or company at a time working your way through the "gate-keeper" (the receptionist), to find the "connector" (the person who knows the interworking of the organization). From there, you find the true "decision maker(s)."

Use your unique understanding of data and trends to communicate what differentiates your product or service from the competition. Create a presentation to show how your product or service can solve problems they currently have, and problems you see coming down the pike. Emphasize how your solution will save them time and money, or their company. Once they agree, start with a test case then scale slowly from there to insure you or your company can handle the increasing volume. When you have a proven sales cycle, find technical solutions to create efficiency and scale to other companies or industries.

Prior to the recession in the late 2000's I was working as a Real Estate Agent in Denver, Colorado. One day in January, I received an interesting phone call. A woman named Dianna was calling from Orlando, Florida, where she worked for a company that did asset management for the Veterans Administration. Dianna asked me if I could provide a valuation on a home that they had foreclosed on and were preparing to sell. She explained she had called several real estate agents, but none of them were interested in providing a value nor helping to even sell property. When she gave me the address of the property, I explained to her that it was located outside the area I typically worked in, but I would look into it anyway.

The property was located in the center of Colorado. The home, or mobile home I should point out, sat on forty acres. The home and land together were not worth much more than $75,000. But this wasn't the actual issue. The bigger issue was the property was located over an hour and a half away from any major city, and in the center of the Rocky Mountains.

It was January in the middle of one of the strongest snow seasons Colorado had seen in a while. Dianna was born and raised in Florida. She had no concept of how large the Rocky Mountains were or how difficult they can be to traverse during winter, much less during a snowstorm. To add difficulty, the property was located near the center of forty acres and

Strategist

had been vacant for months. Nobody shovels snow on the long narrow dirt driveways of vacant mountain properties. I guarantee the road was impassable. When I explained this to Dianna, she was very grateful. I took the time to provide her with a better understanding of the property when all the other real estate agents she had contacted simply dismissed her.

But I saw her request as an opportunity. I asked Dianna which agents her company currently worked with to assist in the sale of homes they managed in the Denver area. She said they had over twenty agents throughout Colorado, but admitted it was difficult and stressful to manage them all. I asked if her company considered working with just two or three agents to eliminate so many different people and processes. Dianna didn't think it was possible, but said she would talk to her supervisor, Mike. "Ah, Mike, the decision maker." I thought.

I took a leap of faith and wrote a fifteen-page proposal on how I would manage listing and selling the properties they managed throughout Colorado. I explained in detail what Dianna had told me, that managing multiple agents, their processes and their attitudes was inefficient and unsustainable. I explained that I would lose money on the $75,000 mountain properties so I would need to have all the listings in the state to make up the difference. It was a bold request.

I sent the unsolicited proposal to Dianna and asked her to send it to Mike. Then I waited. And waited. I left messages with Mike. No response. Days went by, then weeks, then months. But I continued to contact Dianna and Mike.

Then one day I got a call,

"Sean?" a man's voice said.

"Yes?" I replied.

"This is Mike."

"Eureka!" I thought!

I used a big picture approach to identify an opportunity, networked through the connector (Dianna) for the opportunity to meet the decision maker (Mike). I presented what pain points I had been told and how I could solve them by creating a unique solution. Within the few years I worked with Mike and Dianna, my team and I sold over 600 homes.

Other Sales Strategies to consider
The Strategists shares similar personality traits with the **Debater**, **Advisor**, and **General**. We suggest considering those Sales Strategies also.

MBTI: INTJ

Debater

Traits

Internally Focused: The Debater uses their internal focus to analyze ideas or situations and develop solutions or theories.

Logical: They place logic above everything else.

Curious: They are intensely curious about theories, ideas and how things work.

Critical: Debaters listen for illogical and redundant arguments and are not worried about letting you know if you made an error in your communication.

Values
Accuracy
Autonomy
Competence
Intelligence

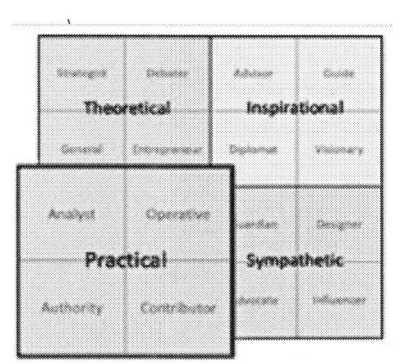

Description

　　A master of the intellectual world the Debater enjoys talking about abstract concepts and principals. Highly intelligent, they have the ability to find solutions to complex problems others cannot solve. Appearing shy and timid, they can be easily underestimated, much to the opponent's dismay. Debaters are masters of language. They do not miss a single point in negotiations, and wait for any opportunity to point out laws in their opponent's logic and argument.

Debater

Competitive and driven, Debaters are also skilled in organization. They do not enjoy routine tasks, but if given a difficult problem they can remain focused for hours until they understand the underlying principal or logical structure. Like game pieces on a game board, they almost see the world and people as raw materials and tools to be molded into whatever vision the Debater wishes to create.

Due to their inner focus and lack of need for many relationships, Debaters may be difficult to get to know. Compared to other personality types, this makes them relatively poor at reading others body language and emotions. Debaters can get lost in their intellectual world and get caught up over analyzing alternatives, which often delays making decisions until it is too late. Additionally, they often waste time considering unrealistic options.

Strengths
- Independent thinking
- Creative problem-solving
- Competitive
- Hungry for knowledge
- Highly intelligent

Weaknesses
- Inability to communicate effectively
- Difficult to lead
- May be impractical
- Lack of respect for others' opinions
- Can be critical of others

Debater

Opportunities

Seek an environment with autonomy and independence for you to be able to create and build your own system or structure. Rely on building the system. Find technology and outsourcing, or delegating to others around you to run the daily routine tasks, so you can keep your focus on learning and growth. Time-block each week with "Time to Think" and "Time to Execute." This will help with the analysis paralysis trap.

When goal setting, manage your desire to stretch to your vision too large. Big goals are great but can become unmotivating if they take too long to achieve. Keep 90-day, 180-day and 6-month milestones to keep focused on the road ahead.

Avoid

Avoid directly managing others, find a business partner or second in command to act as a buffer between your raw, direct thoughts and the sensitive people you are leading. Avoid the desire to jump from project to project, typically due to boredom. Find ways to hold yourself accountable to complete your projects.

Famous Debaters

Larry Page and Serge Brin (founders of Google)
Dwight D. Eisenhower
Marie Curie
Carl Jung

Debater Sales Strategy

Your logical side will direct you to find an efficient solution to generate qualified leads. The solution should be system based, not people based. Dealing with the emotional side of managing people will likely lead to stress and frustration.

Marketing Lead Funnels are a marketing-based system that allows you to strategically target customers by geographic and demographic identifiers. Targeted direct response marketing will funnel potential customers through a series of marketing pieces and questions until the customer shows signs that they are ready to purchase. This is when you will contact, and convert, your leads.

Marketing Lead Funnels are an ideal solution for the Debater. They allow you to use your creativity to find unique solutions. Additionally, this strategy will allow you to work behind the scenes creating leads that have self-selected themselves into the lead funnel. Marketing Lead Funnels include: Internet Ads, Facebook Ads, TV Ads, Radio Ads, and Direct Mail.

Yes, I said Direct Mail, a valuable system often overlooked today. Direct mail provides a predictable conversion ratio. Whether it is 400:1, 1000:3, or 2000:7 the measurable results will satisfy your need for a logical return on your investment.

If you were to ask Scott privately, he would tell you that he doesn't enjoy sales. At all. This is strange considering Scott is a top producing Loan Officer. In fact, he actually loves the challenge that comes with structuring loans and finding the best mortgage for his client's unique situation. Scott says, "The more difficult, the better."

Debater

Fortunately, Scott took the time to create a Marketing Lead Funnel that generates plenty of leads. Scott, a former marine, has specifically designed his marketing strategy around other veterans. His ads influence the targeted customer to purchase or refinance with him because he is "one of them."

Once the lead generates an inquiry, his Contact Management Software takes over by following up with emails and marketing specifically designed to build trust. Junior Loan Officers make the initial calls until the customer is ready to formalize a loan application. This makes the process extremely efficient for Scott.

Loan Application is where Scott takes over. He uses his preference for problem-solving to find the best solution for his veteran clients. His clients appreciate Scott's approach to their unique situation and, in turn, they refer their friends and family.

If your strategy requires leading other people, like Scott's, consider finding an Authority or General to work with. Their natural people skills will attract talented people and prevent you from having to directly lead. The General and Authority personalities also have thick skin that can stand up to any criticism you can dish out.

Other Sales Strategies to consider
The Debater shares similar personality traits with the **Guardian, Entrepreneur**, and the **Guide**. We suggest considering those Sales Strategies also.

MBTI: INTP

General

Traits

> External Focused: The General places their external focus the logical analysis of the situation. Always with the goal in mind, they are vocal about illogical or inefficient solutions, and can come across as disapproving and critical.
>
> Logical: They place logic above everything.
>
> Big Picture: The General thinks often about how to overcome the challenge ahead or find a solution to a potential problem.
>
> Decisive: Once the decision is made, the General immediately translates the decision into executable plans and mobilizes the people to immediately to start the work.

Values
> Being #1
> Intelligence
> Competence
> Commitment
> Leverage

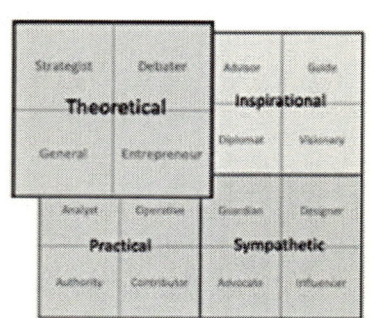

Description

A General's main focus is achievement. With their positive nature and endless drive, Generals attract others that wish to be a part of their mission. Leading others is natural for them, as they see people as soldiers there to help them complete the mission.

General

Generals are concerned with accomplishments rather than the feelings of the people they lead. They surround themselves with loyal and effective workers and they will not tolerate excuses or repetitive errors.

Outgoing and assertive, Generals quickly dominate the conversation, taking their place as the "Alpha." They are honest to a fault. Not concerned with hurting others feelings, they speak and move quickly and when a decision is made. Others are expected to get on board or get out of the way. If they are not part of the mission, they are no longer useful to the General and will be quickly dismissed.

To a General money is an undeniable unit of measurement and accomplishment. Because of this, they are typically top earners, and they will make sure to let you know. Extroverted and inspiring, they also are the first to offer to help others achieve what they, themselves have accomplished.

Generals dislike redundancy, illogical rules, and red tape. If they don't agree with a rule, they will simply ignore it. Justifying that the results are more important than the means. Generals love to challenge the status quo, challenge other leaders and challenge the people they lead. Because great isn't good enough.

Strengths
    Execution
    Natural Leader
    Problem Solver
    Insightful
    Resourceful

Weaknesses

General

Disregards other opinions
Fails to give praise
Unrealistic expectations.
Takes on too much

Opportunities

Look for opportunities where your drive and ambition are seen as an asset and not a liability. Because of your charisma, once you prove your natural ability to sell, you will be asked to lead the sales team. Do not jump at this until you have clearly established short and long-term goals and consider if your direct leadership style will be appropriate for the company's culture.

Avoid

Avoid middle management and underperforming upper leadership. This will cause you stress. Your critical voice, even though you are trying to be helpful, may come across as disruptive and you may be not be seen as a team player. Repetitive tasks that require little mental engagement will be under stimulating and may keep you from achieving your full potential.

Famous Generals

Charlize Theron
General George S. Patton
Margaret Thatcher
George Clooney

General Sales Strategy

Like any Four-Star General your strategy is to create and follow a mission plan. There are five things to consider when building a mission.

Outcome: Begin with the goal in mind. Focus on measurable, short-term sales goals with a long-term vision. Examples include, becoming the #1 Sales Person in the office within the year, #1 in the region in 24 months, then #1 nationally in 36 months. The bigger the goal the bigger the passion. More passion equals more drive!

Remember this is your mission, what have you been called to do?

No mission can be fulfilled without the fuel to fulfill it. Your fuel is your personal passion. Why is it important to you to achieve this goal?

Why are you the one to achieve it?

More than money, what will you gain?

Who will acknowledge you when you achieve your goal?

Goal setting is as simple as building a bridge from where you are to where you want to be. Generals have the tendency to overestimate their abilities and underestimate the difficulty of the task ahead. Therefore, they need to take the time to prepare.

Preparation: To prepare for you mission you will need to research others who have already achieved what you wish to achieve.

General

What resources do they have?

Are you able to acquire the same or similar resources?

What are they doing or have done to achieve it?

What do you need to do or learn to reach your goal?

Threats: Answer this honestly, remember your tendency underestimate the task ahead. "None" is a cop-out answer

Who will prevent you from achieving your goal?

What are the known obstacles that you will need to overcome?

Opportunities: What unique opportunities will help you achieve your goal?

How will you use your unique skills to overcome these obstacles?

Resources: Do you have the resources to achieve your goal?

Time, money and education are all limited by what you have to bring to the table. For large goals, you will need to look to others to provide these resources.

Who can you enlist to help?

Next, formulate your sales process, what activities are you going to do to achieve your sales goals? If you don't already have

General

an effective sales process, review the strategies of the Authority and Entrepreneur for guidance. Add or develop systems to create consistency and accountability. Now you can recruit people to execute your mission!

Other Sales Strategies to consider

The General shares similar personality traits with the **Authority**, **Entrepreneur** and **Diplomat**. We suggest considering those Sales Strategies also.

MBTI: ENTJ

Entrepreneur

Traits

<u>External Focused:</u> The Entrepreneur's external focus is constantly scanning for opportunities to improve the status quo.

<u>Innovative:</u> They can debate ideas for hours until they uncover a strategic plan for implementation.

<u>Rational:</u> Entrepreneurs are able to take a complex problem and find a creative, yet realistic, solution.

<u>Self-Reliant:</u> Strongly independent, the Entrepreneur will use their resourcefulness to come up with the desired result in their own unique way.

Values
Uniqueness
Independence
Intelligence
Efficiency
Respect

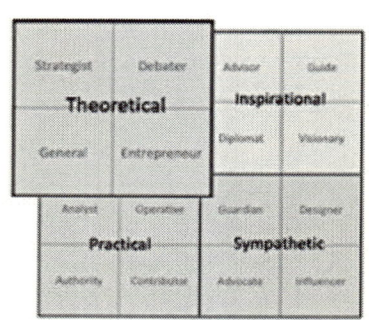

Description

Entrepreneurs are dynamic, motivating and have the ability to inspire others with their ideas and unconventional ways of doing things. When given a difficult problem that piques interest, they will spend endless hours discovering multiple solutions. They are more interested in concepts than traditions or rules.

Entrepreneur

Outgoing and friendly they quickly find people to lead, but often fail at long-term leadership due to the responsibilities and routine that comes with being in charge. This restricts the Entrepreneur's need for freedom and autonomy.

The Entrepreneur has many interests and jumps from one to another. They will spend time gaining knowledge simply for a deeper understanding of things that interest them. They give little time or thought to things that do not stimulate their interest in the moment.

Entrepreneurs can be difficult to lead in an environment of strict rules and control. They will search for shortcuts and loopholes in order to do things their own unique way. They have the ability to find relationships between seemingly unrelated things and processes, and they desire to change the status quo by improving things in their own unconventional way.

Entrepreneurs may explore multiple careers and resources simultaneously, confusing others about their true intentions. If you want to know what an Entrepreneur is up to, just ask. Their outgoing, open attitude is always willing to share their strategies.

Strengths
    Outgoing
    Action-Oriented
    Enthusiastic
    Innovative
    Stimulated by Challenge

Weaknesses
    Risk-taker
    Ignores Rules

Entrepreneur

Doesn't like Routine
Unpredictable

Opportunities

Seek opportunities that allow a flexible schedule to give you time to research your approach and execute your plans. Take time to write out your strategy completely and explain this to your employer and co-workers in detail. You will thrive in environments that look for new solutions to difficult or unseen problems. Commit to working in one position for a specific period of time. This will give you the permission to move on and relieve the pressure of feeling trapped in a long-term role. Choose to work in project timelines with a focused goal, this will help you maintain your focus and energy.

Avoid

Avoid middle-level management positions where you are required to hold others accountable to routine procedures. This will drain your energy and stifle your creativity. Avoid long-term projects and long-term positions where you know you're not "all-in."

Famous Entrepreneurs
Jon Stewart
Barack Obama
Nikola Tesla
Amy Poehler

Entrepreneur Sales Strategy

Your rational desire to find the most efficient and effective Sales Strategies and your irrational need to improve upon them makes it a challenge to offer one, single Strategy. Your strong preference to do things your own unique way will result in you not wanting to follow someone else's plan, or dismissing what is tried and true (unless you are under a great amount of personal or financial stress. This is when a proven, detailed plan is the best thing for you).

The best strategies I can offer are the most effective and efficient techniques for consistent results. We know you will take them and tweak them into something that will work for you. You should know, they probably won't work for anyone else.

With that out of the way, the most efficient sales strategies are Telemarketing and Marketing Lead Funnels.

Efficiency and effectiveness seem to work in opposition to one another. For instance, in persuasive communication, email is highly efficient. You can send 2000 emails in less than a minute, yet you may only get 4-5 responses. And of those responses you will have little chance of persuading them to do much of anything. Sending emails is efficient, but low on the effective scale.

On the other hand, a face-to-face strategy is highly effective. Since 75% of communication is body language, this gives you the best chance to persuade potential clients. However, making 100 sales calls face-to-face can be exhausting, if not impossible. Rendering this method effective, but not efficient.

Efficiency is defined as the amount of personal time spent in relation to the return. Considering this, Telemarketing is still, by far, the greatest return on time spent. Even with caller ID and the "Do Not Call Registry," Telemarketing is still king. You simply cannot do any sales activity that costs less, allows you to demographically and geographically target a specific audience and you can do all of it in your pajamas.

Second to Telemarketing is Marketing Lead Funnels. These are attractive because you watch the local baseball game while leads are dropping into your sales funnel. But when you look at the cost of creating, advertising and managing these systems, it is difficult to get started if financial resources are a concern.

Since I have already done the research on what the most efficient sales strategies are, you can just focus on how to make them unique and effective. There are three ways to take something efficient but ineffective, and make it efficient <u>and</u> effective:

Find a unique strategy, offering or process that only you can provide. What is something that you or your organization can provide that your competition cannot? Find a new, technology, or system and leverage it before it becomes mass market. What new technology can you use before it becomes mainstream?

Use a common tool in an uncommon way but… <u>DON'T SHARE IT.</u>

Sean received his real estate license at the age of twenty-one. He was driven to succeed and possessed the desire to be the Top Agent in his office. His challenge was that he was the same age as the kids of his customers. The average home seller did not take him seriously.

Entrepreneur

One day Sean came across a new home community that was selling brand new homes for less than the price of homes sold forty years earlier. Sean was fascinated by this, so he did more research. He met with the builder of the community who explained that sales were slow. They believed that buyers were not interested in this new style of home because it didn't offer the two-car garages or basements that were common in the area.

There is a light bulb here — Sean had an idea!

He ran an advertisement in the For-Rent section of a local paper that looked something like this:

STOP RENTING
BRAND NEW HOME
3 Bedroom, 2 Bathroom, Garage
Own Less Than Rent
$1000 Down*
$1200 a Month*
(*Required legal Disclosures)

The home builder had been advertising the price and features of the homes but had little response because the other homes in the area offered more features for the same price. Sean ran a contrary ad to attract a new pool of buyers—current renters. He used a common tool, the For Rent section of the newspaper, in an uncommon way. The result was outstanding. Sean sold 27 homes in that single neighborhood all off of that one ad.

The ad continued to work for several years until others began to copy it. To combat competition Sean made his ad larger, and even larger, until cost rendered them ineffective based on the financial return. Sean had to come up with a new strategy.

Did you figure it out? Yes, I am an Entrepreneur. Sean is me.

Other Sales Strategies to consider
　　The Entrepreneur shares similar personality traits with the **Visionary**, **Debater** and **General**. We suggest considering those Sales Strategies also.

MBTI: ENTP

Authority

Traits

<u>External Focused:</u> The Authority places their external focus on organization of projects, operations, procedures and people.

<u>Organized:</u> They have an objective and logical approach to organizing everything in their lives and work.

<u>Real World:</u> The Authority is focused on the realistic and practical approach to getting visible, tangible and measurable results.

<u>Results Oriented:</u> More than anything the Authority wants to see real results. They won't stand for excuses, inefficiency, or disorganization.

Values

Efficiency
Competence
Results
Appreciation

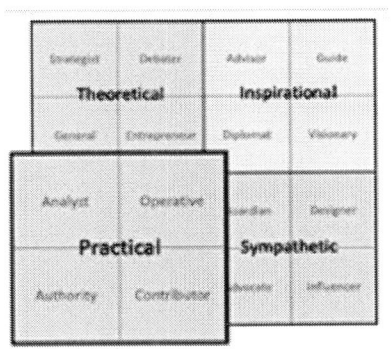

Description

"Results, Results, Results," this is the Authority's mantra. Authorities are seemingly designed at birth to organize and lead missions, projects and people. Confident in themselves, they need little supervision and will create their own procedures and schedules. They are the "take charge and get things done" personality.

Authorities have high standards and strive to exceed other people's expectations. They get started right away and finish early because they despise procrastination. Authorities can be hard on others that do not fall in line with the plan or procedure.

Outgoing, well-spoken and driven all come to mind when talking about the Authority. These traits are appreciated in most organizations and other personality types are often envious of their value and embrace the Authority personality. Authorities prefer predictable schedules with little distraction and hands on tasks that produce tangible, measurable results.

Strengths
    Responsible
    Competent
    Organized
    Direct
    Decisive

Weaknesses
    Inflexible
    "Know-it-all"
    Impatient
    Tough-minded

Opportunities
    Seek opportunities where your straightforward communication and desire for high quality and efficiency are seen as an asset, otherwise you may be labeled as nit-picky. You will thrive in a well-organized environment with scheduled tasks and

clear goals. Take time to review your company's outcomes and bring yours in-tow. This will insure your attention and efforts are appreciated. Your personality is well suited for sales. In fact, you probably are already a top earner in your organization.

Avoid

Be aware that your personality can takeover less dominant personalities. If you want others to buy into your plan, they need to feel heard. You have a tendency to focus too hard on one thing or short-term goals. Take a step back from your efforts once a week and look at the bigger picture. Other personality types who do not do things the way you would will frustrate you. If you wish to become an effective leader you will need to learn to embrace the differences of others.

Famous Authorities
    Judy Scheindlin (Judge Judy)
    Simon Cowell
    Condoleezza Rice
    Alec Baldwin

Authority Sales Strategy

You want it all from your sales strategy— efficient, effective, predictable, proven and ensured results. In sales, efficiency and effectiveness are on different ends of the spectrum. The most efficient sales strategy is email. You can send ten thousand unsolicited emails in just one click, but the results are poor. On the other hand, face to face is the most effective, but the time it takes to go door-to-door, drive or fly just to make your introduction is too inefficient for you. Your need predictable results, so a strategy that has already been tried and true, one that you will get immediate feedback of your effectiveness, is right for you. You have already guessed what it is— the phone.

Today, Telemarketing includes text, direct messaging (DM), and outbound calls. What Actions are you executing each day to create predictable results? An Action is a text, DM, or call. Each Action will produce a Contact. A Contact is someone who answered the phone or responded to you text or DM. Each Contact will provide a Response. Responses can only be one of three categories;

> Interested
> Not Interested
> Not Now

No matter what other pleasantries or colorful word combinations you may hear, these are the only true responses. If you receive no answer, this is not a Response.

Actions, Contacts and Responses are all Key Measures. Key Measures are the areas in your business where you can track the activities and results that lead to the eventual sale. They give an organization a clear idea of the direction their business is moving. Additional Key Measures include Leads, Contacts and Follow Ups. Appointments Set, Presentations Given, and Contracts or Sale made. Think about the sales process as a chain. If you are not getting the results you desire, there is always a break in the chain.

Authority

A break can be something that is not being done or just an area that needs to be improved. Without tracking there is no way to identify where the break is. You may be outstanding at your presentation but poor at your lead conversion. If you do not record your Key Measures it is nearly impossible to find the break in the chain. Therefore, it is challenging to improve performance and effectiveness.

Actions		25
Leads		5
Goal	X	25
Sub Total		**3125**
Weeks	/	45
Actions / Week		**70**

Set your annual goal, break down the goal into Actions you will do each week.

Begin with your goal in mind, how many widgets do you wish to sell each year?

How many Actions do you need to get one Lead?

How many Leads to get one Sale.

Authority

    Multiply Actions by Goal: (Leads x Goal) x Actions = Subtotal

    Divide by 45 Weeks. (45 Weeks worked each year)

    Divide Subtotal by Weeks. (Subtotal/Weeks)

    Time-block your Lead Generation. Protect this time. Do not allow interruption. Record your Key Measures and review them weekly with your supervisor or Coach. Look for areas of improvement, make necessary adjustments and repeat.

Other Sales Strategies to consider

    The Authority shares similar personality traits with the **Analyst**, **Advocate** and **Contributor**. We suggest considering those Sales Strategies also.

MBTI: ESTJ

Contributor

Traits

<u>External Focused:</u> The Contributor lives in the moment and is interested in everything going on around them.

<u>Troubleshooter:</u> Highly rational and energetic. Enjoys finding new methods to solve problems and make work fun.

<u>Observant:</u> Acutely aware of their surroundings. including people, relationships and nonverbal communication.

<u>Reactive:</u> Ready to jump right in and get started knowing they will adapt to whatever comes their way.

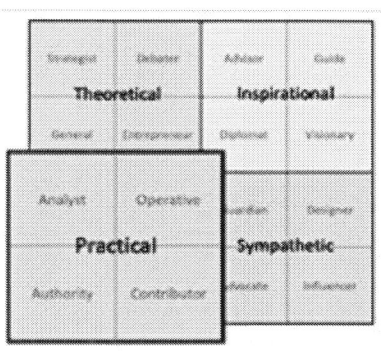

Values
Passion
Direct
Hands-on Experience
Flexibility

Description

  The life of the party, Contributors plunge into anything that offers a new experience. They are observant of their environment and interested in fashion, food and people. They don't allow rules or traditions slow them down, they find creative ways around them instead. Problem solving is their superpower.

  A Contributor will jump in and get their hands dirty. Why would they sit in a class when they can learn by doing? Flexible

Contributor

and good natured makes then great organizers of people, and even better at resolving conflict.

Contributors have little use for conversations about theories or existential ramblings or deep analysis in statistical or analytical nature. These conversations will quickly bore them. They are quick witted with a direct sense of humor and have little sympathy for others around them with thin skin.

Repetition will bore Contributors and they may find themselves changing an effective approach simply because they were bored. The key to their success is keeping active with new experiences. Contributors find success talking to and meeting people. Every new person is a new opportunity.

Strengths
    Great organizers of people
    Good natured
    Adventurous
    Creative problem solving
    Willingness to jump in and figure it out

Weaknesses
    Distracted with enjoying life
    Forgets responsibilities
    Not good at committing to a schedule
    Risk Taker

Opportunities
    Your strengths will shine when you are face to face with your clients. Your quick wit and flexibility allow you to bob and weave around obstacles. Find an organization that will give you a flexible schedule so you can separate work-time from play-time.

Clear boundaries and expectations alleviate misconceptions about your commitment to the organization.

Avoid

Avoid situations that do not allow your creative problem-solving. Rigid schedules with limited time off may will make you unmotivated and disincentivized. Make an arrangement with your yourself or supervisor stating that when you achieve your milestones, you can take extra time off. This will allow you to set short-term goals and manage your energy by working in bursts, and then recharging your batteries with play-time.

Famous Contributors
   Taylor Swift
   Madonna
   George W. Bush
   Bruce Willis
   Malcolm X

Contributor Sales Strategy

Your thick skin and objective outlook allow you to not take things personally. Your adaptable and carefree attitude is perfect for customer direct sales. You have the ability to read people and your persuasive personality style is sure to win others over.

Anthony was new to the area and wanted to get his business started quickly. Anthony offered haberdashery services at affordable prices. Like most new businesses, he didn't have a large marketing budget. He had to find an affordable solution that would give him the best chance for success.

Contributor

Anthony's business was located in a high net worth suburb ten miles from the next major city. The total population was nearly 60,000 with roughly 20,000 residential doors. Anthony noticed successful politicians canvasing neighborhoods in order to build name recognition and to gain the public's trust. This gave Anthony an idea.

Doing simple math Anthony surmised that he could knock on 150 doors a day, three days a week. This meant he could knock on every door in town in less than a year. Anthony could also make a greater impact by showing his efforts on social media. Within a few months the local newspaper featured an article on Anthony, highlighting his mission to knock on every door in town!

Door to Door sales will keep you actively in front of new people. Door to Door can include homes, businesses, offices, etc. Each new door requires you to use your strategies and good humor to make a new friend.

Doors			5
Conversations		X	10
Goal		X	50
Sub Total			**2500**
Weeks		/	45
Actions / Week			**56**

1. Begin with your goal in mind, how many widgets do you wish to sell each year?
2. How many doors do you need to visit to have one conversation?
3. How many conversations do you need to have to sell one widget?
4. Multiply Doors and Conversations. (Doors X Conversations) x GOAL= Subtotal)

5. Divide by 45 Weeks. (45 Weeks worked each year)
6. Divide Subtotal by Weeks. (Subtotal / Weeks)

Use a goal setting tool like this to manage your expectations. Set a standard to do a minimum number of Actions (Doors) each week. Remember your play-time is contingent upon you achieving your results. Share your standards with your peers, manager or coach to help hold you accountable.

Your scripts, posture, consistency and attitude will all contribute to improving your conversion ratios. As you gain experience you will be able to visit less doors and achieve the same results. Use your problem-solving skills and creativity to find the best ways for you to improve your results.

What you don't measure you cannot manage. Be sure to keep track of all your lead generation activities, leads and results. The money is in the follow-up

Other Sales Strategies to consider

The Contributor shares similar personality traits with the **Authority**, **Advocate** and **Operative**. We suggest considering those Sales Strategies also.

MBTI: ESTP

Analyst

Traits

Internal Focus: Focuses on the task or system at hand rather than individuals.

Analytical: Thoroughly analyzes each situation using logical criteria based on their personal experience and knowledge.

Pragmatic: Practical, realistic and matter-of-fact, wants to be seen as "the voice of reason."

Structured: Works within a structured, scheduled approach. "No time for dreamers."

Values
Dependable
Logical
Traditional
Loyal

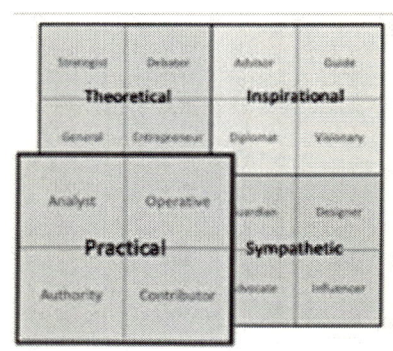

Description

For an Analyst, "get the job done, on time and follow the rules", is the order of the day. With a low tolerance for risk and a strong desire for stability, the Analyst is the most reliable of all personality types. Like soldiers, Analysts are respectable toward hierarchical organizational structures. In fact, they thrive in them.

Analysts are not flashy. They tend to lean towards the tried and true. No need for the latest and greatest, if it isn't broken, don't

Analyst

fix it or replace it. Analysts have rules for every situation. They will not cut corners or take short cuts, but they will ensure the job is completed correctly and on time... the first time.

Analysts will choose large, stable organizations that can fulfill their need for security. If a company provides the stability they desire, they will stay for their entire career. Not one to take risks, they may become stubborn when asked to try something new. Any reason to step outside the lines must be proven to them by someone they trust.

Strengths
> Dependable
> Systematic
> Hard-working
> Follows Rules
> Reliable

Weaknesses
> Averse to taking risks
> Inflexible
> Critical of others
> Has difficulty delegating

Opportunities
> Look for organizations with a tried and true history and a clear organizational structure. Learn about your company's heritage and specific details about your product or service. Follow a clear plan for success with realistic expectations. For presentations, request a detailed schedule and written description, including exact scripts or dialogue. Ask to shadow other successful salespeople whose example you can emulate.

Avoid

Avoid start-up organizations with little experience or structure and high-pressure sales or situations that require immediate results. Focus on mastering the process and not on making the sale. Avoid a "doomsday" approach in your communication as this may push your customers to rethink their decision completely.

Famous Analysts
- Natalie Portman
- Warren Buffet
- Henry Ford
- Jeff Bezos (Founder of Amazon)

Analyst Sales Strategy

Become an expert in your industry by showing off your written communication skills in detailed newsletters, LinkedIn articles, and topical emails. Your wealth of factual observations regarding your product, industry and competition will be valued by your customers and they will come to see you as an expert.

Use a topic schedule to prevent topic indecision. Below is a topic schedule developed for a real estate agent.

Analyst

	Date	Topic
January		
	7th	What is the difference between an Appraisal and Inspection?
	14th	How much downpayment do I need to buy a home?
MLK Day	21st	What fees do I have to pay to sell my home?
	28th	What is the difference between an FHA and Conventional Loan?
February		
	4th	How long does it take to sell a home?
	11th	Do I have to use a Realtor to sell a home?
Pres-Day	18Th	What is rent to own?
	25th	How do I get approved for a loan?
March		
	4th	Why is my assessed value different than the appraised value?
St. Pats	11th	How long does it take to buy a home?
	18Th	What is a back-up offer?
	25th	How do I buy a forclosed home?
April		
	1st	How do I negotiate the best price?
	8th	What is mortgage insurance?
Easter	15th	How do I pick an agent to sell my home?
	22nd	How much do I pay a Realtor to buy a home?
	29th	What is the home sale process?
May		
Mother's Day	6th	What do I do if I miss a house payment?
	13th	How does a VA Loan work?
	20th	Do I have to sell my home before buying another one?
Memorial Day	27th	How do you buy a brand new home?
June		
	3rd	Is staging really effeective?
Father's Day	10th	Do I need a home warranty?
	17th	What is the best ways to market my home?
	24th	How accurate is the Zilow estimate?
July		
4th of July	1st	What is the difference between a Realtor and a real estate agent
	8th	Do national real estate companies have better exposure?
	15th	Do I have to move twice to sell my home and buy another?
	22nd	What is title insurance?
	29th	How do I get an appraisal?
August		
	5th	What are the best sites to search for homes?
	12th	Are all mortgage company interest rates the same?
	19th	Should I do a 15 or 30 year mortgage?
	26th	Does new windows increase the value of my home?
September		
Labor Day	2nd	What home expenses can I write off on my taxes?
	9th	5 low cost things you can do to get more money for your house?
	16th	How does an agent come up with the sales price?
	23rd	What does owner/seller carry mean?
Rosh Hashanah	30th	How much are closing costs?
October		
	7th	How do I get/find the lowest interest rate?
	14th	Are the prices negotiable?
	21st	What is a seller's market?
Halloween	28th	How long does it take to buy a home?
November		
	4th	What kind of credit score do I need to buy a home?
Veteran's Day	11th	What is earnest money?
	18th	Do I need a final walk through?
Thanksgiving	25th	Can a seller reject an offer?
December		
	2nd	How long does it take to sell a home?
	9th	When is the best time to sell a home?
Hanuhah	16th	What do I have to disclose to buyers?
X-Mas	23rd	Why are commissions soo high?
New Years	30th	How long should a listing agreement last?

Analyst

Send you articles and newsletters to other influential experts or organizations and request to become a contributor to their, magazines, podcasts, social groups, etc. Organizations are often looking for a fresh perspective on industry topics.

For additional resources on this strategy I suggest the book *Connect*, by Josh Turner,* which lays out a detailed plan to develop leads using this same strategy on LinkedIn.

Other Sales Strategies to consider
The Analyst shares similar personality traits with the **Authority, Operative** and **Conductor**. We suggest considering those Sales Strategies also.

MBTI: ISTJ

Connect, The Secret LinkedIn Playbook To Generate Leads, Build Relationships, And Dramatically Increase Your Sales. Written by Josh Turner

Operative

Traits

<u>Internally Focused</u>: The Operative's internal focus is on the information, facts and data. They are constantly sorting, organizing and reasoning with themselves.

<u>Critical</u>: Operatives may seem agreeable but internally they are analyzing the situation and making judgements.

<u>Pragmatic</u>: They see themselves as realists, focusing on what can be done rather than theoretical possibilities.

<u>Adaptable</u>: Operatives are ready to respond to whatever the world throws at them.

Values
Facts
Logical Analysis
Independence
Adventure
Competency

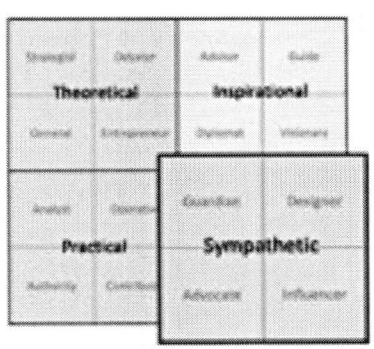

Description

Quiet and reserved, the Operative watches for the right opportunity to jump in and take advantage of the situation. They are always analyzing people, processes and their environment. They have a 'live and let live' attitude, but this does not apply to their judgement of others. They have high standards for their co-workers, leadership and mates.

Operative

Operative are more interested in what can be done than what is possible. They place importance on efficiency of effort and strive for accomplishing any task with minimal effort. They can be action-oriented, flexible, and a risk-taker, often enjoying extreme sports.

They communicate more through their actions and participation than verbally. When they share, they don't share openly, only to a few close friends that share the same interests. They can be an important piece to a team for their keen eye on what is not working, who's not stepping up, and what other people's perceptions are.

Strengths
- Adaptable
- Observant
- Troubleshooter
- Objective Analysis

Weaknesses
- Critical
- Quiet
- Cynical
- Postpone Decision

Opportunities

Seek opportunities that are in your interest. You will have trouble selling anything you don't actually use. When you believe in it, you will learn all the specifics, what is unique, and how to use it properly. Your passion for the product will become your superpower. When you love it and use it, you will sell it.

Avoid

Avoid products or people you do not believe in, your critical judgement of them will prevent you from passionately selling the product or service. Avoid withholding your opinions and emotions, your observations are a powerful tool to help a company improve redundant processes and inferior products. Be sure to take time to develop trust with your leadership so your feedback is taken as constructive not critical.

Famous Operatives
    Snoop Dog
    Clint Eastwood
    Scarlett Johannsen
    Simon Cowell

Operative Sales Strategy

Your best strategy is finding the ideal customers for the product or service you are selling. Identify these people and prepare a specific presentation, knowing exactly what their challenges, needs and desires are and what objections they may have. The more specific the better. Identifying a niche customer will save you time, effort and money. Find specific customers that everyone else is overlooking and you will make a fortune!

Strategically position yourself to meet that specific demographic face to face. Yes, face to face. You will be more natural face to face than over the phone or by email. Networking, trade shows and events will position you in front of your target audience.

Operative

Describe your target customer:

Demographics:
- _____ Age
- _____ Location
- _____ Home-Owner or Renter
- _____ Gender
- _____ Income level
- _____ Education level
- _____ Marital or family status
- _____ Occupation
- _____ Position

Psychographics:
- _____ Personality
- _____ Attitudes
- _____ Values
- _____ Interests/hobbies
- _____ Lifestyles
- _____ Behavior

Are there enough people who fit my criteria?

Will my target really benefit from my product/service?

What is their need or desire? (Symptom)

Why do they have those needs or desire it? (Cause)

Can they afford my product/service?

Can I reach them with my message and are they easily accessible?

Operative

What are three difficult situations my target customer faces?

    1.
    2.
    3.

What are three solutions my product or service provides?

    1.
    2.
    3.

What are three reasons they may not take action?

    1.
    2.
    3.

What are three solutions to these objections?

    1.
    2.
    3.

    When you meet your potential customer you will only have a few seconds to grab their attention. Prepare a thirty second attention getting introduction specific to this target customer. Consider what your target customer needs and what you can offer that will grab their attention?

"Are you interested in learning about the latest technology in…?"

"I have a list of homes that are not on the market yet, would you like to see it?"

"If I could show you how to save forty hours a month would that interest you?"

Once you have their attention, ask them to watch or attend a short presentation that will speak to their needs specifically. You will need to create a 15-20 minute presentation that will specifically solve your target customer's challenges and fulfill their needs. And, don't forget to ask for the sale.

Other Sales Strategies to consider
The Operative shares similar personality traits with the **Analyst**, **Guardian**, and **Contributor**. We suggest considering those Sales Strategies also.

MBTI: ISTP

Advocate

Traits

    External Focused: The Advocate directs their focus on meeting the needs of the people they care deeply about.

    Warm: Friendly, sympathetic and caring by nature, they practically radiate warmth.

    Traditional: The Advocate enjoys the celebration and community of traditions, such as birthdays, anniversaries and holidays.

    Organized: They prefer structured situations and enjoy bringing order, if it doesn't exist already.

Values

    Harmony
    Traditions
    Organization
    Connection

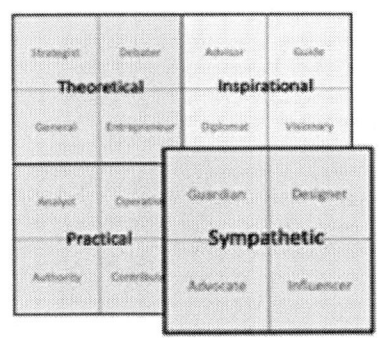

Description

    Advocates work hard to show the people they care about that they are thought of and loved. The Advocates primary driver is their concern for what their loved ones think of them. All they seek in return is their love and appreciation.

    All of the Advocates actions are in the service of others with little concern for their own needs. Their decisions are based more

Advocate

on how they might affect others than logic or efficiency The Advocate believes traditions are relevant because they remind us of the important things in life.

Advocates are not motivated by material possessions, awards or money. They are more concerned with harmony and being seen as helpful. It is not to say that they cannot, or will not be successful. Many Advocates are outstanding salespeople, they are simply not doing it for the money.

Advocates can become stubborn and unmotivated if they are not receiving the adoration they truly desire. They will become doubtful, worrisome and may feel guilty. This can leave them feeling slighted, even when the offense was not intended.

Strengths

    Outgoing
    Nurturing
    Loyal
    Hospitable
    Dutiful

Weaknesses

    Overly concerned with the approval of others
    Dislikes Conflict
    Worry and Guilt
    Sensitive

Opportunities

Find an organization, product, or service you truly believe serves people. You will not be able to sell something you do not believe will help your customers. Lean into your strength of building community. Once you find the right organization, product or service, focus your attention on demographic or geographic target audiences where can build community.

Avoid

Avoid organizations that place the importance of the sale over the customer. This will lead to guilt and stress for you. Remind yourself that you do not need approval from all your customers. Seek out your tribe, the people that care about the organization, product or service in the same way you do. The others are simply not your tribe. No judgement, just let it go.

Famous Authorities

Martin Luther King Jr.
Jennifer Lawrence
Emma Stone
Barack Obama

Advocate Sales Strategy

You are going to worry about looking "Salesy." This feeling may slow you down. Remember every good company, product or service you love was sold by someone. For you, sales is not manipulation, it is sharing something you deeply believe in. Let your sales come from a place of contribution and service.

Building a community around your desire to improve you customers lives, businesses and finances is the best strategy for you. There are two ways to accomplish this specific technique depending on the physical location of your customer.

Demographic Community: A community based on specific people or positions that would benefit from your product or service. Not, businesses or industries in general, you want to target the people that make the decisions. For instance, if you are selling Payroll Management services you could be looking for the owners, hiring managers and human resource of start-up and small companies.

Ask yourself:

What specific situations are causing them to lose money, earn less money, lose time, or making their lives less enjoyable?

How can your specific product or service solve this?

Now build your community by reaching out and inviting them to learn more about the specifics of the Payroll Management services you provide. Build a community online via email newsletter, Facebook groups and LinkedIn. Once you have built your online Demographic Community, invite them to an event once a month, quarter or year to develop deeper relationships and build trust.

Geographic Community: A group of people inside a specific area that would benefit from your product or service. If you are selling hazard insurance, begin by focusing all your activities on a specific geographic area. Become the "Face of Insurance" in your area by door-knocking regularly, sending a newsletter offering solutions to the situations specific to each community. Spending money on low-cost marketing and branding specific to the neighborhood.

Start small and develop relationships. One of the most common mistakes people make in marketing is starting with too large of a market area. With Geographic marketing it is important to start small and build influence before spreading out.

First time farmer, Jim, chooses to plant a large 100-acre piece of land. Jim begins by tilling the full 100 acres. This takes six weeks. By the time Jim finishes tilling, weeds have already returned to the first 25 acres and Jim has to go back and re-till. He then rushes to plant his seed, which takes another two weeks. Jim's impatience and hurriedness leaves the land with areas with areas of low seed count. When Jim finally completes his planting, he has spent thousands of hours and tens of thousands of dollars only to find that, by the time his plants began to grow, he had missed the ideal growing season. At harvest his plants were scarce and small. The nights were getting cold and his plants are dying. Jim's fears I that he won't be able to recoup the money he spent.

Across town, Suzy began with a small fertile patch of land not much larger than 20 acres. Since the land was small and manageable, she was able to till and plant in thirty days. Suzy spend her extra time weeding and tending to the weaker plants to insure the best harvest ratio. Her extra attention paid off and her plants grew large and strong during the growing season. Suzy's harvest was ideal and the return on her time and money was highly profitable.

Begin by hosting neighborhood events at your home, in the park or at local businesses. Plan events such as:

- Ice cream social at a local business
- Movie in the park
- Neighborhood garage sale
- Neighborhood shred day
- Holiday pie pick-up
- Neighborhood BBQ
- Neighborhood food-drive

Advocate

Most people make the mistake of believing that the measurement of success for an event is attendance. This is not true. You are not selling tickets to a concert. The true goal is the contacts you make leading up to the event. Your true task is managing the premarketing to the event. If this is done correctly to will develop name and face recognition and create leads for new customers.

Action	How	When
Save the Date	Social Media Posts	4 Weeks Out
Save the Date	Email	3 Weeks Out
Invitation	Mailed Invitation	2 Weeks Out
Personal Call	Phone	7-10 Days Out
Pop-By	In Person	0-7 Days Out
EVENT		
Thank You	Phone	0-7 Days After
Thank You Card	Mailed	1 Week After
Newsletter with Photos	Emailed/Mailed	7-30 Days After

Avoid the desire to expand too quickly into other areas until you have made a full impact in your neighborhood. Over time, you will be seen as the connector in the neighborhood, the one that cares deeply about the needs of the community.

Advocate

Other Sales Strategies to consider

The Advocate shares similar personality traits with the **Guardian**, **Influencer** and **Authority**. We suggest considering those Sales Strategies also.

MBTI: ESFJ

Influencer

Traits

<u>External Focused:</u> The Influencer focuses on meeting the needs of others in creative ways.

<u>Experiential:</u> They are interested in having enjoyable experiences with other people.

<u>Peacemaker:</u> Influencers are great observers of other's emotions, they are empathetic and will respond quickly to the needs of others.

<u>Spontaneous:</u> They seldom plan ahead. They go with the flow trusting they will figure it out as they go. They avoid structure and routine.

Values
Cooperation
Creativity
Harmony
Adventure
Possessions

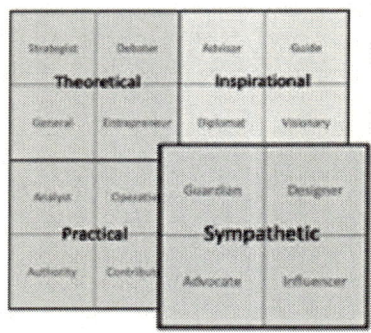

Description

The Influencer focuses on people-first, placing a high value on their time and activities with others. They enjoy food, clothing, nature, animals and activities. They love to mix work and play. They are at their best when spending time with other people.

Influencer

Down to earth, practical and in the moment. They can jump from task to task with or without regard to priority, but they always accomplish the to do list. Schedules and routines are too confining. They may overlook long-term consequences for short-term fun and pleasure.

Caring and warm, Influencers will quickly mobilize people to help others in crisis. They strive to do their best and expect the same from others. They care deeply about other people's feelings and avoid conflict.

Strengths
Friendly
Fun
Cleaver
Flexible
Peacemaker

Weaknesses
Easily Distracted
Dislikes Routine
Sensitive
Trouble meeting deadlines.

Opportunities
Look for opportunities to spend time with your clients and meet new potential customers. Attend industry conferences, seminars and meet-ups anywhere you can learn more about your industry, product or service. Industry and product knowledge will build your confidence. Confidence will support your customer engagement.

Avoid

You may have the tendency to worry about potential negative outcomes. Worrying can propel you into believing you are just not meant to have it, be it or do it. This type of thinking will not serve you, or your goals. When this happens, think of one thing you can do to move closer to what you desire and get into action.

Famous Influencers
John F. Kennedy
Miley Cyrus
Will Smith
Deepak Chopra

Influencer Sales Strategy

With a strong focus on helping others and the ability to mix work and play, find ways to create experiences for your customers that build your Influence while helping others. Think of ways to make doing business with you feel like an experience.

Think of your current client experience from the moment they first make contact with you and throughout the transaction. How can you make the experience magical?

Monica, cares deeply for her family, they are the reason she works so hard. Her second passion is Disney, Disney World to be specific. She decided to take the Disney experience and apply it to her business. Like Disney World, every customer experience has been meticulously thought out to ensure that experience is second to none. Working with Monica is the same experience. Monica teaches other Real Estate Agents how to create a Disney experience in their business.

Influencer

You can visit Monica's website at: www.theagentofexcellence.com.

Connect your "why" to your passion to help others and your product or service. Orchestrate an amazing experience for your customers from the moment they inquire, through the sales cycle, until the end of your career. Through creating happy experiences for your customers, you will feel like you've never worked a day in your life.

Other Sales Strategies to consider:
The Influencer shares similar personality traits with the **Guide**, **Advocate** and **Designer**. We suggest considering those Sales Strategies also.

MBTI: ESFP

Guardian

Traits

Internal Focus: The Guardian's internal focus is on the wealth of information they have collected over their lifetime. They have the ability to recall specific details and events because each hold a special meaning.

Specific: They are practical, detailed and concrete in their use of language. They are drawn to subjects that are practical and need clear and detailed direction.

Sacrificial: The Guardian's duty is to serve and protect the people they care about, even if it goes against their own self-interest.

Dependable: They place a high priority on completion and following through on all tasks and responsibilities.

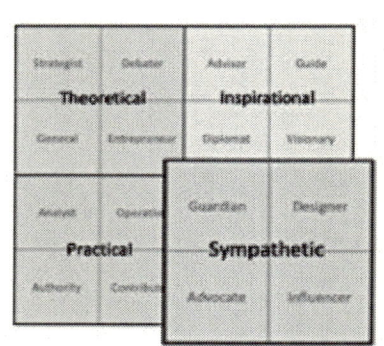

Values
   Details
   Kindness
   Responsibility
   Loyalty

Description
   Guardians are committed to the people, communities and groups they are associated with. They will go to great lengths to

fulfill the needs of their people and will sacrifice their time, money and lives to serve and protect the people they care about. They make clear decisions based on facts, experiences and inner core values. They respect established procedures and authority, especially when it supports their personal communities. They can become rigid to change if they cannot see any practical benefit to people.

Guardians prefer to operate behind the scenes. They do not step into the spotlight even to take credit for their accomplishments. They avoid confrontation at all costs. Due to this, they may withdraw from a situation. They can be accommodating, even when they disagree with the matter at hand.

Strengths
    Selfless
    Literal
    Organized
    Considerate
    Humorous

Weaknesses
    Self-sacrificing
    Dislikes change
    Takes criticism personally
    Strong dislike of conflict.

Opportunities
Your product, service or organization must serve the good of the people, community or society as a whole. Your connection to this cause is vital for you to feel committed to your work. Your depth of information will serve your organization well. Spend time

Guardian

learning the facts and details about your industry, product or service your competition overlooks.

Avoid

Avoid catastrophizing situations and outcomes, this will repel your customers. Focus on positive outcomes. Avoid withdrawing from the organization, team or group when conflict arises. They need your knowledge even if they don't immediately show appreciation.

Famous Guardians
- Halle Berry
- Mother Teresa
- Jimmy Carter
- Rosa Parks
- Tiger Woods

Guardian Sales Strategy

Your natural tendency is to avoid looking and acting like a traditional salesperson. However, providing information that can save a potential customer from making a mistake that will cost them money, time and frustration is your Superpower. With your preference for introversion you will need to place yourself where others can readily access your knowledge of your product or service.

You will find trade shows and booths outstanding sales strategies. To manage trade shows you must be organized, prepared and friendly. These traits don't commonly go hand-in-hand for most, but they do for you. Trade shows and conventions are events created specifically to an industry, demographic or topic. Your potential customers will attend trade shows as guests to gain training, inspiration and networking.

A booth is typically at an event that serves a community, like a community Harvest Festival or holiday parade. These events are not specific to an industry or demographic, they are more commonly associated with a holiday, season or specific event. Look for opportunities to rent a booth and share information or make direct sales at these types of events.

Your goal for both tradeshows and booths is to meet potential customers, collect contact information and develop relationships by utilizing your vast knowledge. Here are some specific tips to insure your tradeshow and booths are successful.

Branding: Take time to develop your specific brand. If you are in a service industry like Insurance or Real Estate, your face is your brand. Your booth and must be visible from forty feet away and should reflect your brand.

Social Media: Prior to the event, begin promoting on Facebook, Twitter, LinkedIn and Instagram. Let people know where your tradeshow or booth will be and how to find you. Continue to promote on social media during the entire event.

Organization: Review the event location and be strategic about the location of your booth. Visibility is a necessity. Events are not always as prepared as you are so plan on arriving early to set up. This will give you time for last minute printing or to chase down a promised extension cord. Collect all contact information with an IPAD or tablet to ensure the information is not lost. Additionally, you can have an automated email sent immediately, so they have your contact information, as well. Keep a notepad to quickly jot down names, company and notes from your conversations. This will help trigger your memory when you follow up.

Products: People are attracted to products. When they see you have beautiful, well-branded products or swag (slang for inexpensive giveaways), they will curiously approach your booth.

Giveaways: If you are selling products, hand out inexpensive samples— a t-shirt, sticker, postcard or prototype. If you are selling services, give away your knowledge with books, pamphlets and presentations.

Goals: As I said before, your main goal is to meet potential customers and collect their contact information in order to develop relationships. In my experience, setting goals for your time at a tradeshow or booth increases contacts and contact information by over fifty percent. When we are intentional about why we are there, we waste less time, meet more people, help more people and build relationships. Set goals around talking to potential customers, collecting data and making a sale. All of this should be measured, recorded and reviewed.

Be Present, Friendly and Welcoming: We have all been at tradeshows and have seen the person behind a booth not making eye contact and looking uninterested. She might be truly passionate about her product, but at that moment, she was drifting off and thinking about other things. It takes effort to stay focused and remain present, friendly and welcoming. Make eye contact with each person, smile as if you just saw an old friend for the first-time, in a long time, and say hello to everyone. This will keep your mind from wandering into La La Land.

Follow up, Follow up, Follow up: You are happy because you've had a successful event and met several people who were interested in your product or service. Yet, when you begin to contact them, they seem disinterested. This is where your unique wealth of knowledge takes over. Send them an email one a week or add them to a campaign that provides important, detailed information. Follow up with a call to see if they have any questions regarding the information you send. There is no need to sell, you are simply becoming a trusted source for information. When they are ready, they be sure and contact you because of your vast knowledge of the industry, product or service.

Other Sales Strategies to consider
   The Guardian shares similar personality traits with the **Designer**, **Contributor** and Advocate. We suggest considering those Sales Strategies also.

MBTI: ISFJ

Designer

Traits

Internal Focus: The Designer focuses their attention on finding inner joy and happiness.

Strong Core Values: They have clear values that they live by and demonstrate those values through their actions.

Factual: The Designer pays close attention to the realities of the present and is observant of the people and the world around them.

Independent: They are warm, caring and independent. They balance between the two worlds of connecting with others and enjoying their private time.

Values
   Harmony
   Empathy
   Loyalty
   Privacy

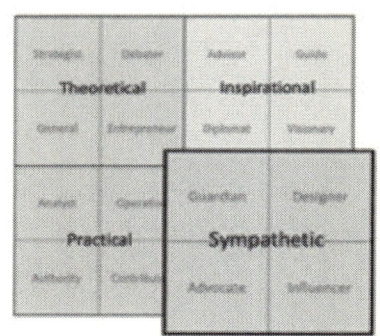

Description

Designers are happiest when they are creating. They yearn for the time and freedom to express themselves through their creations. This is why so many are musicians, actors and artists. They appreciate the simple beauty of nature, music, food and art.

Designer

They are accommodating, loyal and friendly, even when they disagree. Designers are attuned to the feelings of others, they seek opportunities to contribute to the well-being of those around them. It may take longer to get to know a Designer, but once they develop a relationship, that relationship becomes very important.

Designers learn through hands on experience, not by reading or listening. They prefer to get involved in the activities and learn as they go. If Designers are not able to use their creative side, they may withdraw or feel unappreciated. This may present itself as harsh criticism of themselves, and possibly others.

Strengths
>Warm
>Loyal
>Cooperative
>Adaptable
>Tolerant

Weaknesses
>May seem disinterested.
>Self-critical
>Resist Structure
>Can feel unappreciated.

Opportunities
>Look for organizations, products or services that are more than just one transaction. Your strong ability to preserve relationships will serve you well but, due to your introverted nature, it may take you longer to develop new relationships. Repeat clients, service contracts and subscriptions will allow you to become successful by simply managing fewer relationships over a lifetime.

Designer

Avoid
Avoid organizations, products and services that you do not believe in. Your caring nature will not allow you to sell something you don't see beneficial to the customer, the community or society.

Famous Designers
Paul McCartney
Barbara Streisand
Ulysses S. Grant
Beyoncé Knowles

Designer Sales Strategy

Your superpower is in your caring nature and deep connections with people. Specifically, one person at a time. You make people feel nurtured, needed and special. Your Strategy must reflect the importance of developing true relationships with your customers, and not just the transaction.

Use your creative side to create low cost, unique gifts that you can give your customers. It may be a book you find interesting, a special gift made specifically for them, or it can be as simple as a coffee mug filled with candy.

Your unique gift will become the reason to "pop by". Maybe you were just in the area or happened to be out for a special occasion. This strategy gives you the internal permission you need to visit customers unannounced. You can pop-by their home, their office or even their job-site. No excuses. Nobody gets upset when you are bringing them a gift, I promise.

Designer

The best technique is preparation. Have baskets, coffee mugs or other gifts premade and ready for delivery. Watch social media for opportunities to pop-by. Anniversaries, birthdays and holidays are all reasons to show that you care. Don't spend a lot of time with small talk, just let them know you were thinking of them and wanted to bring them a gift. Your only objective is to ask them if they may be available in the near future to get together for a coffee, lunch, dinner, etc.

Your goal is to develop deeper relationships with each of your customers. If your product or service is more business related, selling copy machine services, for instance, you may simply do coffee or a quick lunch. If your product or service is more relational, I suggest inviting them to dinner at your house or playing eighteen holes of golf.

Show your customers how much you care about them as a person by asking what challenges they may facing. Your natural, transparent and caring nature will take over and they will feel your honest warmth and trust. Trust develops relationships.

Brenda was a veteran loan originator when she was introduced to the number one Realtor in the city. Brenda had her doubts. She asked herself, "Why would he want to work with me?" This Realtor probably worked with plenty of loan originators already. But, Brenda stayed out of her head and kept in action. She walked into the Realtor's office and asked to speak with him. Fortunately, he was available for a quick minute. He was busy, focused and polite. Brenda expected his to be arrogant and dismissive. She was pleasantly surprised.

Instead of asking directly for him to refer his loans to her, she tried a different approach. She said, "I don't expect you to refer me right away.

Designer

But, I would like to learn more about you and how I might be of service. What is the greatest challenge you are facing today?"

The Realtor was quiet for a moment. "I just opened a new Real Estate Brokerage, but I don't really have the business experience to run it. I need to learn how to run a Brokerage." Brenda paused, took down the note and replied, "Let me see what I can come up with."

Brenda returned a week later with a big grin on her face. "You are right," she said. "It is challenging to find information on how to run a Real Estate Brokerage, but I did find these books." Brenda set a stack of books on the Realtor's desk. Some of them were over thirty years old. It was obvious that Brenda had spent some time looking for these resources.

That was the beginning of a business relationship that lasted for over ten years. Brenda came from a place of service. She used her creativity to develop trust, and a new friendship.

Any guess who the Realtor was?

Other Sales Strategies to consider
The Designer shares similar personality traits with the **Influencer, Operative** and **Guardian**. We suggest considering those Sales Strategies also.

MBTI: ISFP

End

Congratulations on committing to learning more about your unique personality type and wanting to understand others' innate preferences. This is the start of beautiful friendships, partnerships, collaborations— and of simply taking care of yourself.

There is a wealth of information, opportunities and success available out there. Your new self-awareness will open doors you never knew existed. Holding this book means you have a goal. At least one, could be many.

At 16 Strategies, our goal is to help you along your journey. As you get closer to each finish line, we will be here cheering you on. We are always happy to answer questions, provide information and clarify knowledge.

We offer coaching and support from one on one sessions and assessment, to corporate training—and for everyone in between.

Let us know how we can help!

Visit us at
16strategies.com

About the Author

Sean Moudry has a track record of success from entering the REMAX Hall of Fame by the age of 24, featured in REALTOR Magazine 30 Under 30 (2002), recognized nationally as a top producing real estate agent for over 15 Years consistently. Leading Keller Williams Realty franchise offices through the downturn and recruiting over 115 agents in a single year, landing in the top ten nationally and #1 commercial KW office (2011).

Founding a real estate brokerage in Boulder Colorado, within four years STEPS Real Estate had become one of the fastest growing real estate companies in Colorado, with four locations across the front range. STEPS was featured in Real Producers Magazine and a Reality TV show Buying Boulder. Steps Real Estate joined the cloud-based Brokerage eXp Realty to provide opportunity to the agents.

When you think of Sean think passion, enthusiasm, and authenticity. Having coached and trained over 3000 Agents and Mortgage Professionals throughout the Unites States, his inspiring stories and relentless drive for personal growth makes for a dynamic experience.

For speaking inquiries please visit:
16strategies.com

Made in the USA
Columbia, SC
18 June 2020